"The Bible's narrativ‹ ... em-
bedded in Genesis 3 ... con-
textualized by the wa〉‿ ...._.. ... man.
But the end of the story is promised from the beginning: although the serpent
grows large into a fierce dragon, its head is finally crushed by a Lion who,
even before creation, was destined to become a slain Lamb. This conflict is
not Scripture's only unifying theme, but it is a fundamental one, and Andy
Naselli highlights it wonderfully. He provides us with a key that will open
the door to a new appreciation of the sheer thrilling nature of what God has
done for us in Christ. Prepare, then, to be thrilled by *The Serpent and the
Serpent Slayer!*"

    Sinclair B. Ferguson, Chancellor's Professor of Systematic Theology,
    Reformed Theological Seminary; Teaching Fellow, Ligonier Ministries

"Noted biblical scholar Andy Naselli draws readers into the biblical story
through a fresh vantage point—snakes! In this enjoyable book there is consid-
erable insight into Satan, the fall, Christ's victory, and our future."

    Christopher W. Morgan, Dean and Professor of Theology, California
    Baptist University; author, *Christian Theology*; editor, Theology in
    Community series; coeditor, *ESV Systematic Theology Study Bible*

"Knowing our enemy is important. Read this if you want to understand the
schemes of the serpent seen throughout Scripture. But even more importantly,
we must know the serpent slayer. Read this if you want to see how Jesus defeats
the dragon and rescues his bride. What a Savior!"

    Abigail Dodds, author, *(A)Typical Woman*

"Snakes deceive; dragons devour! But the serpent slayer is greater still! This book
traces the hope of the gospel from the garden in Genesis to the new Jerusalem
in Revelation. It identifies the deceptive and devouring purposes of the serpent
in Scripture's storyline, but it magnifies how the Old Testament anticipates and
the New Testament realizes the victory of Christ for and through his church.
This book models well how to trace a biblical-theological theme through the
whole of Scripture, and it is infused with hope in the one who triumphs through
great tribulation."

    Jason S. DeRouchie, Research Professor of Old Testament and Biblical
    Theology, Midwestern Baptist Theological Seminary

"In this slim book, Andy Naselli does what he does best: he gathers, organizes, and presents Scripture so that you can see for yourself what the Bible says about serpents and the serpent slayer. The Bible's understanding of snakes and dragons is 'thick'—it is woven into the fabric of redemptive history from Genesis to Revelation. If you love stories where the hero kills the dragon to get the girl, then this book is for you."

Joe Rigney, Assistant Professor of Theology and Literature, Bethlehem College & Seminary; author, *The Things of Earth* and *Strangely Bright*

"Dragons and serpents have fascinated the human race from time immemorial, whether in secular or sacred literature. In *The Serpent and the Serpent Slayer*, Andy Naselli fascinates us again with intriguing observations and exegetical insights. Every reader will benefit from this concise biblical theology, understanding afresh that while the Bible is a simple story—as simple as 'Kill the dragon, get the girl!'—it is also of dramatic interest from start to finish. Naselli also provides us with a timely reminder that the devil is real and active today, deceiving and devouring people; yet the church is not without hope: Christ has crushed the serpent, and one day so too will his church."

Jonathan Gibson, Associate Professor of Old Testament, Westminster Theological Seminary

The Serpent and the Serpent Slayer

Short Studies in Biblical Theology

Edited by Dane C. Ortlund and Miles V. Van Pelt

The City of God and the Goal of Creation, T. Desmond Alexander (2018)

Covenant and God's Purpose for the World, Thomas R. Schreiner (2017)

Divine Blessing and the Fullness of Life in the Presence of God, William R. Osborne (2020)

From Chaos to Cosmos: Creation to New Creation, Sidney Greidanus (2018)

The Kingdom of God and the Glory of the Cross, Patrick Schreiner (2018)

The Lord's Supper as the Sign and Meal of the New Covenant, Guy Prentiss Waters (2019)

Marriage and the Mystery of the Gospel, Ray Ortlund (2016)

Redemptive Reversals and the Ironic Overturning of Human Wisdom, G. K. Beale (2019)

The Serpent and the Serpent Slayer, Andrew David Naselli (2020)

The Son of God and the New Creation, Graeme Goldsworthy (2015)

Work and Our Labor in the Lord, James M. Hamilton Jr. (2017)

The Serpent and the Serpent Slayer

Andrew David Naselli

WHEATON, ILLINOIS

The Serpent and the Serpent Slayer

Copyright © 2020 by Andrew David Naselli

Published by Crossway
        1300 Crescent Street
        Wheaton, Illinois 60187

Cover design and illustration: Jordan Singer

First printing 2020

Printed in the United States of America

Trade paperback ISBN: 978-1-4335-6797-1
ePub ISBN: 978-1-4335-6800-8
PDF ISBN: 978-1-4335-6798-8
Mobipocket ISBN: 978-1-4335-6799-5

Library of Congress Cataloging-in-Publication Data

Names: Naselli, Andrew David, 1980– author.
Title: The serpent and the serpent slayer / Andrew David Naselli.
Description: Wheaton, Illinois : Crossway, [2020] | Series: Short studies in biblical theology | Includes bibliographical references and index.
Identifiers: LCCN 2019059527 (print) | LCCN 2019059528 (ebook) | ISBN 9781433567971 (trade paperback) | ISBN 9781433567988 (pdf) | ISBN 9781433567995 (mobi) | ISBN 9781433568008 (epub)
Subjects: LCSH: Serpents in the Bible. | Dragons in the Bible. | Serpents—Mythology. | Dragons—Mythology. | Christian life—Biblical teaching.
Classification: LCC BS1199.S37 N37 2020 (print) | LCC BS1199.S37 (ebook) | DDC 220.6/4—dc23
LC record available at https://lccn.loc.gov/2019059527
LC ebook record available at https://lccn.loc.gov/2019059528

Crossway is a publishing ministry of Good News Publishers.

BP		30	29	28	27	26	25	24	23	22	21	20
15	14	13	12	11	10	9	8	7	6	5	4	3	2	1

To my daughter Kara,
who loves serpent-slaying stories
that echo the greatest story

Contents

Series Preface

Most of us tend to approach the Bible early on in our Christian lives as a vast, cavernous, and largely impenetrable book. We read the text piecemeal, finding golden nuggets of inspiration here and there, but remain unable to plug any given text meaningfully into the overarching storyline. Yet one of the great advances in evangelical biblical scholarship over the past few generations has been the recovery of biblical theology—that is, a renewed appreciation for the Bible as a theologically unified, historically rooted, progressively unfolding, and ultimately Christ-centered narrative of God's covenantal work in our world to redeem sinful humanity.

This renaissance of biblical theology is a blessing, yet little of it has been made available to the general Christian population. The purpose of Short Studies in Biblical Theology is to connect the resurgence of biblical theology at the academic level with everyday believers. Each volume is written by a capable scholar or churchman who is consciously writing in a way that requires no prerequisite theological training of the reader. Instead, any thoughtful Christian disciple can track with and benefit from these books.

Each volume in this series takes a whole-Bible theme and traces it through Scripture. In this way readers not only learn about a given theme but also are given a model for how to read the Bible as a coherent whole.

We have launched this series because we love the Bible, we love the church, and we long for the renewal of biblical theology in the academy to enliven the hearts and minds of Christ's disciples all around the world. As editors, we have found few discoveries more thrilling in life than that of seeing the whole Bible as a unified story of God's gracious acts of redemption, and indeed of seeing the whole Bible as ultimately about Jesus, as he himself testified (Luke 24:27; John 5:39).

The ultimate goal of Short Studies in Biblical Theology is to magnify the Savior and to build up his church—magnifying the Savior through showing how the whole Bible points to him and his gracious rescue of helpless sinners; and building up the church by strengthening believers in their grasp of these life-giving truths.

Dane C. Ortlund and Miles V. Van Pelt

Preface

This book is a biblical theology of snakes and dragons—especially *the* serpent. It may be helpful to state up front three beliefs I presuppose in this book:

1. The Bible is God-breathed, entirely true, and our final authority.[1]
2. We must read any part of the Bible in light of the unified, noncontradictory whole. We might focus on a section of the Bible such as the Pentateuch or the entire Old Testament, but ultimately we must interpret any part of the Bible in its fullest literary context. At this stage in the history of salvation, when we read any part of the Bible—such as the episode of the serpent's deceiving the woman in Genesis 3—we must read with *Christian* eyes,[2] with a whole-Bible canonical approach.[3]

---

1. See D. A. Carson, ed., *The Enduring Authority of the Christian Scriptures* (Grand Rapids, MI: Eerdmans, 2016). For a more popular-level approach, see Andrew David Naselli, "Scripture: How the Bible Is a Book like No Other," in *Don't Call It a Comeback: The Same Faith for a New Day*, ed. Kevin DeYoung (Wheaton, IL: Crossway, 2011), 59–69.

2. See D. A. Carson, "Current Issues in Biblical Theology: A New Testament Perspective," *Bulletin for Biblical Research* 5, no. 1 (1995): 40–41.

3. See Douglas J. Moo and Andrew David Naselli, "The Problem of the New Testament's Use of the Old Testament," in *The Enduring Authority of the Christian Scriptures*, ed. D. A. Carson (Grand Rapids, MI: Eerdmans, 2016), 702–46; Aubrey M. Sequeira and Samuel C. Emadi, "Biblical-Theological Exegesis and the Nature of Typology," *The Southern Baptist Journal of Theology* 21, no. 1 (2017): 11–34.

3. Biblical theology is a fruitful way to read parts of the Bible in light of the whole. Biblical theology studies how the whole Bible progresses, integrates, and climaxes in Christ. That is, it is a way of analyzing and synthesizing the Bible that makes organic connections with the whole canon on its own terms, especially regarding how the Old and New Testaments integrate and climax in Christ.[4]

I mention those three presuppositions because many biblical scholars reject them and consequently interpret parts of the Bible much differently than I do in this book. A good example is Professor James Charlesworth, who taught New Testament at Duke University 1969–1984 and at Princeton Theological Seminary 1984–2019. His 744-page tome on serpents took him six years to research.[5] His book is a treasure for its detailed research on what serpents could symbolize in the ancient world, but Charlesworth's main argument is feasible only if the above three presuppositions are false. His main argument is that serpent symbolism is primarily *positive* not only in the ancient Near East but also in the Bible, specifically that Jesus is the serpent in John 3:14 ("As Moses lifted up the serpent in the wilderness, so must the Son of Man be lifted up"). More on John 3:14 later.

———

I thank the following friends for contributing to this book:

1. My mentor Don Carson fanned into flame my love for studying how the whole Bible progresses, integrates, and climaxes in Christ.

---

4. See Jason S. DeRouchie, Oren R. Martin, and Andrew David Naselli, *40 Questions about Biblical Theology*, 40 Questions (Grand Rapids, MI: Kregel, 2020).

5. James H. Charlesworth, *The Good and Evil Serpent: How a Universal Symbol Became Christianized*, The Anchor Yale Bible Reference Library (New Haven, CT: Yale University Press, 2010).

2. My colleague Joe Rigney gave me penetrating feedback as I prepared to research this book and after I drafted it. We almost decided to coauthor it, but he was preoccupied with other projects. Rigney coined the pithy phrase "Kill the dragon, get the girl!"[6] He actually ignited my interest in this topic. In 2013, he emailed the Bethlehem College & Seminary faculty with a list of topics on which he thought our ThM students might want to consider writing their theses. One of the topics he suggested was a biblical theology of snakes and dragons. I've wanted to write this book ever since.

3. Dane Ortlund and Miles Van Pelt warmly welcomed this volume into their Short Studies in Biblical Theology series. Those two men deeply love the triune God. It's so evident in their humility and ministry. (Miles also inspires me to do strength training. His biceps are as large as a python that just swallowed a caiman.)

4. Phil Gons, my close friend for nearly two decades and who is currently vice president of Bible study products at Faithlife, helped me use Logos Bible Software to study serpents efficiently and thoroughly.

5. Some friends graciously offered feedback on drafts of this book, including Charles Ackman, Brian Collins, Jason DeRouchie, Abigail Dodds, Scott Jamison, Jeremy Kimble, Marty Machowski,

---

6. It started with Dane Ortlund's article that asked twenty-six scholars and pastors to summarize the Bible in a single sentence. See Dane Ortlund, "What's the Message of the Bible in One Sentence?," Strawberry-Rhubarb Theology, January 12, 2011, https://dogmadoxa.blogspot .com/2011/01/whats-message-of-bible-in-one-sentence.html. Rigney was intrigued with Doug Wilson's sentence: "Scripture tells us the story of how a Garden is transformed into a Garden City, but only after a dragon had turned that Garden into a howling wilderness, a haunt of owls and jackals, which lasted until an appointed warrior came to slay the dragon, giving up his life in the process, but with his blood effecting the transformation of the wilderness into the Garden City." That led Rigney to summarize the Bible with the phrase "Kill the dragon, get the girl!" He started including that tagline to the end of his emails, and his friend Doug Wilson loved it. Now on Saturday nights when Wilson asks his grandchildren a round of catechism questions, his last question is "Kids, what's the point of the whole Bible?" The kids answer, "Kill the dragon, get the girl!" See Douglas Wilson, *Writers to Read: Nine Names That Belong on Your Bookshelf* (Wheaton, IL: Crossway, 2015), 144. Wilson's publishing house even published a children's novel with that title: Cheston Hervey and Darren Doane, *Kill the Dragon, Get the Girl* (Moscow, ID: Canon, 2015).

Charles Naselli, Matt Rowley, Mark Ward, and Matthew Westerholm. Special thanks to my teaching assistants, Matt Klem and Noah Settersten, for their detailed feedback.

6. My wife, Jenni, supports the research-writing-teaching-shepherding ministry to which God has called me. This project fascinated her, and she helpfully suggested ways to improve the book. She and our daughters also encouraged me to turn this book into a children's book.[7]

7. Andrew David Naselli and Champ Thornton, title to be decided (Greensboro, NC: New Growth, forthcoming in 2022).

Introduction

Why We Love Dragon-Slaying Stories

Who doesn't love a good dragon-slaying story? There is a reason that classic literature features such stories—we love them! But why?

Dragon-Slaying Stories Echo the Greatest Story

We love good dragon-slaying stories because they echo the greatest story—the grand story of the Bible. Stories that parallel the greatest story make our hearts soar with delight. Those stories are often fiction, such as Tolkien's *The Lord of the Rings*. Epic stories resonate deeply with us because they echo the greatest story. And the greatest story is true.

A pithy way to summarize the Bible's storyline is "Kill the dragon, get the girl!"[1] The storyline features three main characters:

---

1. See my footnote 6 about that phrase in the preface (p. 15). "Kill the dragon, get the girl!" is not a misogynist saying or a cavalier cowboy phrase. It colorfully reflects classical literature like *Saint George and the Dragon* and the Bible itself. Jesus decisively defeated the dragon, and he will conquer the dragon and save his bride: "Husbands, love your wives, as Christ loved the church and gave himself up for her" (Eph. 5:25); "Come, I will show you the Bride, the wife of the Lamb" (Rev. 21:9). The metaphor doesn't communicate every nuance (e.g., God helps his people fight the serpent), but it communicates a prominent biblical theme in a pithy way.

1. The serpent (the villain—Satan)
2. A damsel in distress (the people of God)
3. The serpent slayer (the protagonist and hero—Jesus)

The serpent attempts to deceive and devour the woman, but the serpent slayer crushes the serpent.

Serpent is an umbrella term that includes both snakes and dragons. It's the big category. Snakes and dragons are kinds of serpents. The Greek word δράκων (*drakōn*), explains an expert Greek linguist, refers to "a monstrous serpent"—"the ancients Greeks did not visualize it as a winged, fire-blowing creature with claws."[2]

A serpent has two major strategies: *deceive* and *devour*. As a general rule, the form a serpent takes depends on its strategy. When a serpent in Scripture attempts to deceive, it's a snake. When a serpent attempts to devour, it's a dragon. Snakes deceive; dragons devour. Snakes tempt and lie; dragons attack and murder. Snakes backstab; dragons assault (see table 1).

Table 1. The strategies of snakes versus dragons

Snakes	Dragons
deceive	devour
tempt	attack
lie	murder
backstab	assault

Here's how the greatest story unfolds:

- The story begins with bliss. The damsel enjoys a beautiful garden in a pristine world. (Adam and Eve enjoy the garden of Eden.)

---

2. Moisés Silva, ed., "Δράκων," in *New International Dictionary of New Testament Theology and Exegesis*, 2nd ed., 5 vols. (Grand Rapids, MI: Zondervan, 2014), 1:774.

- But the serpent employs the strategy to deceive, tempt, lie, and backstab. (The snake deceives Eve.)
- As the story develops, the serpent craftily alternates between deceiving and devouring. (For example, sometimes Satan attempts to deceive God's people with false teaching. At other times Satan assaults God's people with violent persecution.)
- At the climax of the story, the dragon attempts to devour the hero but fails. (The dragon murders Jesus but merely bruises Jesus's heel while Jesus decisively crushes the serpent's head.)
- For the rest of the story, the dragon furiously attempts to devour the damsel. (The dragon attempts to deceive and destroy the church.)
- The hero's mission: kill the dragon, get the girl. He will accomplish that mission. (The Lamb will consummate his kingdom for God's glory by slaying the dragon and saving his bride.)

That story never gets old.

Six Dragon-Slaying Stories That Echo the Greatest Story

Fiction is filled with dragons.[3] In what follows, I highlight six of the most popular dragon-slaying stories in English literature.[4] These stories echo the greatest and true story. (*Spoiler alert:* The following summaries highlight some turning points in the plotlines.)

---

3. See "List of Dragons in Literature," Wikipedia, https://en.wikipedia.org/wiki/List_of _dragons_in_literature.

4. Cf. Joseph Campbell's thesis regarding the hero's journey in classic literature: Joseph Campbell, *The Hero with a Thousand Faces*, 3rd ed. (Novato, CA: New World Library, 2008). The British journalist Christopher Booker labels one of the seven basic plots of literature as "overcoming the monster." See Christopher Booker, *The Seven Basic Plots: Why We Tell Stories* (London: Continuum, 2004).

Saint George and the Dragon

A staple children's book in our home is an illustrated version of *Saint George and the Dragon*.[5] It adapts the legendary story from Edmund Spenser's epic poem *The Faerie Queene*,[6] which flows from legends about King Arthur such as *Sir Gawain and the Green Knight*. This is the classic dragon-slaying story in English literature.

Saint George was a Roman soldier who died as a Christian martyr in 303. Later traditions venerated him as a legendary dragon killer. The story has many variations in different countries and cultures, but this is the gist: A dragon terrorizes a community, which offers sacrifices to the dragon in order to access water to survive. (In some versions of the story, the people sacrifice all their farm animals and then desperately resort to sacrificing their children!) The dragon's next victim is a royal young lady. A knight (e.g., Saint George or Arthur) arrives on his horse, and the community's spirit transforms from despair to hope. The knight slays the dragon and thus saves the damsel. Then the knight marries her.

How does that story echo the greatest story? "The thief comes only to steal and kill and destroy" (John 10:10). Satan, the devouring dragon, is the ultimate thief who terrorizes God's image bearers. The dragon's next victim after Christ is the church, the bride of Christ (Rev. 12). A knight will arrive on a white horse (Rev. 19:11) to defeat the dragon (19:11–20:15) and rescue his bride (19:7).

Beowulf[7]

Beowulf is an epic Old English story that may be as old as the 700s. A monster named Grendel is slaying warriors at night in the mead

---

5. Margaret Hodges, *Saint George and the Dragon* (New York: Little, Brown, 1984).

6. See Edmund Spenser, *Fierce Wars and Faithful Loves: Book I of Edmund Spenser's "The Faerie Queene,"* ed. Roy Maynard (Moscow, ID: Canon, 1999).

7. *Beowulf: A New Verse Rendering*, trans. Douglas Wilson (Moscow, ID: Canon, 2013); *Beowulf*, trans. Stephen Mitchell (New Haven, CT: Yale University Press, 2017).

hall of the king of the Danes over a twelve-year period. Beowulf, a Scandinavian prince, arrives and heroically slays Grendel with his bare hands by ripping off Grendel's arm. The next night another monster—Grendel's mother—attacks the hall to avenge her son, and Beowulf decapitates her with a sword he finds in her cave under a lake.

Beowulf later reigns as king of his own people for fifty peaceful years, but then a dragon terrorizes his realm. Beowulf slays the dragon with the help of Wiglaf, one of his men, but the dragon mortally wounds Beowulf, who gives his life for his people.

How does that story echo the greatest story? Satan and his minions are monsters who seek to destroy God's people. Jesus unselfishly and sacrificially fights the monsters, and he gives his life for his people.

THE PILGRIM'S PROGRESS[8]

The Pilgrim's Progress is one of the bestselling books of all time. Its author, John Bunyan (1628–1688), was an English Puritan preacher who started to draft the allegory while he was in prison for preaching without the Church of England's sanction. The famous preacher Charles Spurgeon read *The Pilgrim's Progress* over one hundred times.

The allegory features a pilgrim named Christian who perseveringly journeys from his hometown, the City of Destruction, to the Celestial City. He starts off with a great burden on his back, and the burden falls off at the cross. He encounters many obstacles on his journey, including one with a dragon named Apollyon. Leland Ryken, professor emeritus of English literature at Wheaton College, argues that this horrifying serpent is likely "a composite of details that [Bunyan] found in his acquaintance with fictional chivalric romances and

---

8. John Bunyan, *The Pilgrim's Progress from This World to That Which Is to Come*, ed. C. J. Lovik (Wheaton, IL: Crossway, 2009).

in various parts of the Bible, including the description of Leviathan in Job 41 and various monsters in the book of Revelation."[9]

Apollyon is lord of the City of Destruction, and he claims that Christian is his subject. Apollyon accurately accuses Christian of a series of sins, but Christian replies in a disarming way. He basically says: "You're right, Apollyon. I'm actually even worse than that. But the Prince I serve and honor is merciful and forgiving." Christian and Apollyon fight for over half a day, and Christian finally gives Apollyon a mortal thrust with his sword, declaring, "No, in all these things we are more than conquerors through him who loved us" (Rom. 8:37). This key scene in Bunyan's allegory ends with a retreating serpent: "When he heard these words, Apollyon spread out his dragon wings and flew away, and Christian saw him no more."[10]

The King enables Christian to finish the journey. Christian and his companion Hopeful receive a rich welcome (cf. 2 Pet. 1:11) when they enter into the Celestial City and, more importantly, the joy of their Lord.

How does this story echo the greatest story? Jesus mercifully forgives his people of their sins, and he enables them to persevere in the faith. Jesus is the ultimate serpent slayer, and he enables his people to fight the serpent. Christians must put on the whole armor of God so that they can stand against the serpent's schemes (Eph. 6:11–18). "Resist the devil, and he will flee from you" (James 4:7).

THE CHRONICLES OF NARNIA[11]

A seven-book fantasy series for children, The Chronicles of Narnia has sold over one hundred million copies. C. S. Lewis (1898–1963) masterfully tells the story of Narnia from its creation to its consummation.

9. Leland Ryken, *Bunyan's "The Pilgrim's Progress"* (Wheaton, IL: Crossway, 2014), 31.

10. Bunyan, *Pilgrim's Progress*, 92.

11. C. S. Lewis, *The Magician's Nephew* (New York: HarperCollins, 1955); Lewis, *The Lion, the Witch, and the Wardrobe* (New York: HarperCollins, 1950); Lewis, *The Horse and His Boy* (New York: HarperCollins, 1954); Lewis, *Prince Caspian: The Return to Narnia* (New York:

After the lion, Aslan, sings Narnia into existence, the witch, Jadis, attempts to kill the lion by throwing an iron bar at its head. When the bar glances off the unaffected lion, the witch realizes that she is unable to defeat him and runs shrieking into the forest. A boy named Digory is responsible for bringing the witch into Narnia. Aslan explains to the talking beasts: "Before the new, clean world I gave you is seven hours old, a force of evil has already entered it; waked and brought hither by this son of Adam. . . . Evil will come of that evil, but it is still a long way off, and I will see to it that the worst falls upon myself."[12]

"The worst" indeed falls upon Aslan when the witch executes him on the stone table. But Aslan willingly sacrifices himself for Edmund—a son of Adam whom the witch craftily deceived and now plans to devour. The next morning, Aslan rises from the dead, and Edmund's sisters, Susan and Lucy, don't understand how this can be.

> "It means," said Aslan, "that though the Witch knew the Deep Magic, there is a magic deeper still which she did not know. Her knowledge goes back only to the dawn of time. But if she could have looked a little further back, into the stillness and the darkness before Time dawned, she would have known that when a willing victim who had committed no treachery was killed in a traitor's stead, the Table would crack and Death itself would start working backward."[13]

Aslan leads faithful Narnians to defeat the witch and her evil forces: "Then with a roar that shook all Narnia from the western lamp-post to the shores of the eastern sea the great beast flung himself upon the White Witch."[14]

HarperCollins, 1951); Lewis, *The Voyage of the Dawn Treader* (New York: HarperCollins, 1952); Lewis, *The Silver Chair* (New York: HarperCollins, 1953); Lewis, *The Last Battle* (New York: HarperCollins, 1956).

12. Lewis, *The Magician's Nephew*, 148.
13. Lewis, *The Lion, the Witch, and the Wardrobe*, 163.
14. Lewis, *The Lion, the Witch, and the Wardrobe*, 177.

But the witch is not the only person who rebels against Aslan. At least four other types of foes are noteworthy.

1. Some people rebel against Aslan by *cursing him and worshiping other gods*. For example, the Calormenes, from the country Calormen, southeast of Narnia, worship the vulture-headed god Tash in Tashbaan, their capital. After King Lune of Archenland successfully defends his kingdom from a surprise attack from Calormen's Prince Rabadash, King Lune attempts to deal mercifully with his prisoner. But Rabadash curses the king. Then Aslan appears. Rabadash shrieks:

> Demon! Demon! Demon! I know you. You are the foul fiend of Narnia. You are the enemy of the gods. Learn who *I* am, horrible phantasm. I am descended from Tash, the inexorable, the irresistible. The curse of Tash is upon you. Lightning in the shape of scorpions shall be rained on you. The mountains of Narnia shall be ground into dust.[15]

After several unheeded warnings, Aslan humiliates Rabadash by transforming him into a donkey.

2. Some people rebel against Aslan by *being skeptical and selfish*. For example, "There was a boy called Eustace Clarence Scrubb, and he almost deserved it."[16] That gem is the opening line to a book in which Aslan transforms Eustace. "Eustace had read only the wrong books. They had a lot to say about exports and imports and governments and drains, but they were weak on dragons."[17] Eustace changes from an obnoxious brat to a greedy, lonely dragon[18] to a repentant dragon to a relatively pleasant boy. The turning point is when Aslan powerfully and mercifully de-dragons Eustace, who is unable to remove his dragon skin.

---

15. Lewis, *The Horse and His Boy*, 217.

16. Lewis, *The Voyage of the Dawn Treader*, 3.

17. Lewis, *The Voyage of the Dawn Treader*, 87.

18. Cf. the dragons in C. S. Lewis, *The Pilgrim's Regress: An Allegorical Apology for Christianity, Reason, and Romanticism*, 3rd ed. (Grand Rapids, MI: Eerdmans, 1943), 221–27.

It would be nice, and fairly true, to say that "from that time forth Eustace was a different boy." To be strictly accurate, he began to be a different boy. He had relapses. There were still many days when he could be very tiresome. But most of those I shall not notice. The cure had begun.[19]

3. Some creatures rebel against Aslan by *terrorizing humans*. For example, the great sea serpent loops itself around King Caspian's ship to snap it into floating matchwood, but the crew survives by pushing "the snake loop" off the end of the ship.[20]

4. Some people rebel against Aslan by *attempting to deceive his creatures*. For example, the "Lady of the Green Kirtle" encounters Eustace, Jill, and Puddleglum. She is described as riding "on a white horse, a horse so lovely that you wanted to kiss its nose and give it a lump of sugar at once. But the lady, who rode side-saddle and wore a long, fluttering dress of dazzling green, was lovelier still."[21] She deceives the travelers by directing them to shelter with supposedly gentle giants who would actually eat the guests during the autumn feast. It turns out that the beautiful lady is both the evil queen of Underland and the serpent that deceived the long-lost Narnian prince whom the travelers are attempting to save. She has imprisoned the prince by enchanting him with her magic, and when the travelers attempt to free the prince, she almost enchants them to concede that Aslan is not real. But Puddleglum fights off the enchantment, and the witch changes her strategy from deceiving to devouring.

The instrument dropped from her hands. Her arms appeared to be fastened to her sides. Her legs were intertwined with each other, and her feet had disappeared. The long green train

---

19. Lewis, *The Voyage of the Dawn Treader*, 112.
20. Lewis, *The Voyage of the Dawn Treader*, 116–20.
21. Lewis, *The Silver Chair*, 87–88.

of her skirt thickened and grew solid, and seemed to be all one piece with the writhing green pillar of her interlocked legs. And that writhing green pillar was curving and swaying as if it had no joints, or else were all joints. Her head was thrown far back and while her nose grew longer and longer, every other part of her face seemed to disappear, except her eyes. Huge flaming eyes they were now, without brows or lashes. . . . The great serpent which the Witch had become, green as poison, thick as Jill's waist, had flung two or three coils of its loathsome body round the Prince's legs. Quick as lightning another great loop darted round, intending to pinion his sword-arm to his side. But the Prince was just in time. He raised his arms and got them clear: the living knot closed only round his chest— ready to crack his ribs like firewood when it drew tight. . . . With repeated blows they hacked off its head.[22]

How does the story of Narnia echo the greatest story? The Lamb will consummate his kingdom for God's glory by slaying the dragon and saving his bride. At the end of the series, Aslan explains: "The term is over: the holidays have begun. The dream is ended: this is the morning." Lewis continues:

And as He spoke He no longer looked to them like a lion; but the things that began to happen after that were so great and beautiful that I cannot write them. And for us this is the end of all the stories, and we can most truly say that they all lived happily ever after. But for them it was only the beginning of the real story. All their life in this world and all their adventures in Narnia had only been the cover and the title page: now at last they were beginning Chapter One of the Great

22. Lewis, *The Silver Chair*, 183–84.

Story which no one on earth has read: which goes on forever: in which every chapter is better than the one before.[23]

It's difficult to read that last paragraph without tears beginning to form.

THE HOBBIT AND THE LORD OF THE RINGS[24]

The Hobbit by J. R. R. Tolkien (1892–1973), like Narnia, has sold over a hundred million copies; and its sequel, the three-book fantasy set *The Lord of the Rings*, has sold over 150 million copies.

Tolkien formed an extremely detailed background for his story. But here's the gist: The title *The Lord of the Rings* refers to the main villain, Sauron, the dark lord of Mordor. Sauron is the primary serpent figure in the epic story. He has forged a powerful ring to use as the supreme weapon, and a hobbit named Frodo attempts to destroy it.

After Frodo destroys the "One Ring" in the fire of Mount Doom, Frodo and his faithful friend Sam struggle to survive just outside Mount Doom as the area self-destructs. They assume they are about to die. They faint. Two eagles rescue them. Sam later wakes up. He sees a nine-fingered Frodo next to him, and then he remembers everything.

Sam and Frodo don't know what the readers know. They think the wizard Gandalf died way back in the mines of Moria. They don't know Gandalf is alive.

Gandalf informs Sam where he is and asks,

"Well, Master Samwise, how do you feel?" . . .

---

23. Lewis, *The Last Battle*, 210–11.

24. J. R. R. Tolkien, *The Hobbit: or, There and Back Again* (Boston: Houghton Mifflin, 1937); Tolkien, *The Fellowship of the Ring* (Boston: Houghton Mifflin, 1954); Tolkien, *The Two Towers* (Boston: Houghton Mifflin, 1955); Tolkien, *The Return of the King* (Boston: Houghton Mifflin, 1956). For resources on Middle Earth that my family enjoys, see "Ten Resources for Enjoying Tolkien's *The Hobbit* and *The Lord of the Rings*," Thoughts on Theology, October 19, 2012, http://andynaselli.com/ten-resources-for-enjoying-tolkiens-the-hobbit-and-the-lord-of-the-rings.

But Sam lay back, and stared with open mouth, and for a moment, between bewilderment and great joy, he could not answer. At last he gasped: "Gandalf! I thought you were dead! But then I thought I was dead myself. *Is everything sad going to come untrue?* What's happened to the world?"

"A great shadow has departed," said Gandalf, and then he laughed, and the sound was like music, or like water in a parched land; and as he listened the thought came to Sam that he had not heard laughter, the pure sound of merriment, for days upon days without count. It fell upon his ears like the echo of all the joys he had ever known. But he himself burst into tears. Then, as a sweet rain will pass down a wind of spring and the sun will shine out the clearer, his tears ceased, and his laughter welled up, and laughing he sprang from bed.

"How do I feel?" he cried. "Well, I don't know how to say it. I feel, I feel"—he waved his arms in the air—"I feel like spring after winter, and sun on the leaves; and like trumpets and harps and all the songs I have ever heard!"[25]

"Is everything sad going to come untrue?" Answer: Yes![26]

How does the story of *The Lord of the Rings* echo the greatest story? Jerram Barrs suggests several "echoes of Eden" in the story. "The memory of Paradise as it originally was" echoes the good creation. "The loss of Paradise and the sad reality of the present fallen world" echo the fallen creation. "The hope of redemption and the regaining of Paradise" echo the redeemed creation.

---

25. Tolkien, *The Return of the King*, 962–63. Italics added.
26. Cf. Timothy Keller, *The Reason for God: Belief in an Age of Skepticism* (New York: Dutton, 2008), 31–34; Keller, *Walking with God through Pain and Suffering* (New York: Dutton, 2013), 116–18; Michael J. Kruger, "'Is Everything Sad Going to Come Untrue?': Eschatology in *The Lord of the Rings*," Canon Fodder, October 31, 2012, https://www.michaeljkruger.com/is-everything-sad-going-to-come-untrue-eschatology-in-the-lord-of-the-rings/.

Tolkien's story treasures biblical virtues such as humility, serving others, and self-sacrifice.[27]

HARRY POTTER[28]

The seven-book Harry Potter fantasy series by J. K. Rowling (1965–) is the best-selling series in history—over five hundred million copies. While some people think Harry Potter is dark literature that Christians should avoid, I am convinced it is filled with implicit and explicit Christian themes.[29]

The protagonist is Harry Potter, and the main antagonist is Lord Voldemort. Voldemort is the most powerful dark wizard—so dreaded that nearly everyone in the magical community fears to even say his name and instead calls him *You-Know-Who* or *He-Who-Must-Not-Be-Named*. Voldemort's goal is to become immortal and rule both the wizarding world and the Muggle (i.e., non-magical) world. His servants are the Death Eaters, evil wizards and witches. But an unlikely obstacle is in his path—a boy named Harry Potter.

When Harry turns eleven, he learns that he is a wizard—and not just any wizard but a famous one in the magical community. He is famous because Voldemort cast a killing curse on him when he was an infant. Voldemort attempted to murder baby Harry because he understood a prophecy to say that if Harry lived, Voldemort must die. But Voldemort's curse did not harm Harry, because his mother's self-sacrificial love protected him. The curse rebounded

---

27. Jerram Barrs, *Echoes of Eden: Reflections on Christianity, Literature, and the Arts* (Wheaton, IL: Crossway, 2013), 118–24.

28. J. K. Rowling, *Harry Potter and the Sorcerer's Stone* (New York: Levine, 1998); Rowling, *Harry Potter and the Chamber of Secrets* (New York: Levine, 1999); Rowling, *Harry Potter and the Prisoner of Azkaban* (New York: Levine, 1999); Rowling, *Harry Potter and the Goblet of Fire* (New York: Levine, 2000); Rowling, *Harry Potter and the Order of the Phoenix* (New York: Levine, 2003); Rowling, *Harry Potter and the Half-Blood Prince* (New York: Levine, 2005); Rowling, *Harry Potter and the Deathly Hallows* (New York: Levine, 2007).

29. See John Granger, *How Harry Cast His Spell: The Meaning behind the Mania for J. K. Rowling's Bestselling Books*, 4th ed. (Carol Stream, IL: Tyndale, 2006)—*Time* magazine calls John Granger the "Dean of Harry Potter Scholars"; Barrs, *Echoes of Eden*, 125–46.

and hit Voldemort instead. It left a lightning-shaped scar on Harry's forehead, and it disembodied Voldemort. It takes Voldemort over a decade to regain his body and power.

Harry attends Hogwarts School of Witchcraft and Wizardry to learn how to properly use his magical powers. He and his faithful friends Hermione Granger and Ron Weasley survive multiple encounters with Voldemort and his Death Eaters. (Each of the seven novels tells the story of one year of Harry's life, from age eleven through seventeen.)

Rowling's story makes selfish people look repulsively wicked, and unselfish people attractively noble.[30] Voldemort is the ultimate serpent figure in the series. Hogwarts has four houses. Harry is in the House of Godric Gryffindor, whose mascot is a lion; Voldemort was in the House of Salazar Slytherin, whose mascot is a serpent. In the second book, Voldemort opens the "Chamber of Secrets" to unleash a basilisk, a monstrous serpent that can instantly kill living things simply by making eye contact with them. Voldemort is a "Parselmouth"—that is, he has the rare ability to speak Parseltongue, the language of snakes. (Harry also has this ability because of his connection with Voldemort.) Nagini, Voldemort's loyal and terrifying snake, guards Voldemort's immortality. Voldemort is supremely selfish. His main strategies are to deceive and to devour.

Harry's wise and trustworthy headmaster, Albus Dumbledore, explains to Harry that Voldemort has split his soul into pieces and thus created a series of "Horcruxes." The only way to defeat Voldemort is to destroy those Horcruxes. Harry, Ron, and Hermione set out on a quest to destroy the Horcruxes, and near the end of that quest Harry realizes that *he* is one of the final Horcruxes. Because he loves his family and friends, Harry willingly surrenders himself to

---

30. Cf. Granger, *How Harry Cast His Spell*, 15, which displays the good-versus-evil relationships throughout the storyline.

Voldemort and expects to die in order to save the lives of his friends. But when Voldemort again casts a killing curse at Harry, the self-sacrificial Harry enters an in-between state in which he can choose whether to die and go on or to remain alive and try to finish off Voldemort. He chooses to return to fight because he loves his friends. When Harry and Voldemort duel for the final time, Voldemort dies from his own killing curse when his curse rebounds off Harry's defensive spell.

How do you think the story of Harry Potter echoes the greatest story? Here are two hints: (1) Harry defeats Voldemort with self-sacrificing love, and (2) Harry conquers death with his own death.[31]

On to the Greatest Story

Those six dragon-slaying stories echo the greatest story. That's why people love them.

Now on to the greatest story. It begins with God's creating the heavens and the earth as good. But a deceptive snake enters the garden.

---

31. See Barrs, *Echoes of Eden*, 142–44.

1

The Deceitful Snake in Genesis 3

The serpent theme spans the entire Bible—from the beginning of Genesis to the end of Revelation.[1] Let's start with what the Bible teaches about the serpent at the story's beginning. Genesis 3 teaches at least twelve notable truths about the snake.

Here's a clarifying note about an aspect of this book's format: *I quote the Bible a lot.* I do this for two reasons. First, it helps you engage directly with the Bible and not merely indirectly through what I say about the Bible. To help you connect specific God-breathed words with what I am arguing, I italicize portions of direct quotes. Second, it helps you realize, "Wow! The serpent theme is all over the Bible." It is a prominent theme at the Bible's bookends (the beginning of Genesis and end of Revelation) and in between.

The Snake Is Deceitful

Now the serpent was *more crafty* than any other beast of the field that the LORD God had made. (Gen. 3:1)

---

[1]. A logical way to begin studying the serpent theme is to locate all the relevant Bible passages that use various terms for serpent. Laying out that data is a bit technical, so it's an appendix rather than a chapter: "How Often Does the Bible Explicitly Mention Serpents?" If you are more academically inclined, read the appendix before you read chapter 1.

The grand story does not begin with the deceitful snake in Genesis 3. It begins with God's creating the heavens and the earth in Genesis 1–2. The story begins with pure goodness. All is right with the world—until the crafty villain enters the scene.

In English, *crafty* means cunning or deceitful. But *crafty* in Genesis 3:1 translates a Hebrew word that is neutral on its own. It can be positive (e.g., Prov. 12:16—*prudent* as opposed to foolish) or negative (e.g., Job 5:12; 15:5). Here the word is initially ambiguous. But when you reread this story in light of the whole story, *crafty* is an excellent translation. The serpent is the craftiest wild animal. His first strategy is not to devour but to deceive.

The Snake Is a Beast That God Created

> Now the serpent was more crafty than any other beast of the field *that the LORD God had made*. (Gen. 3:1)

God created the snake, so the snake is not God's equal. God is uncreated; the snake is created. Aseity is true only of God—that is, only God exists from himself without depending on anything else for existence.[2] Like every other creature, the snake is not independent of God.

The Snake Deceives by Questioning God

> And the LORD God commanded the man, saying, "You may surely eat of every tree of the garden, but of the tree of the knowledge of good and evil you shall not eat, for in the day that you eat of it you shall surely die." (Gen. 2:16–17)

> He [i.e., the snake] said to the woman, "*Did God actually say*, 'You shall not eat of any tree in the garden'?" And the woman said to the serpent, "We may eat of the fruit of the trees in the

---

2. Cf. John Webster, "Life in and of Himself: Reflections on God's Aseity," in *Engaging the Doctrine of God: Contemporary Protestant Perspectives*, ed. Bruce L. McCormack (Grand Rapids, MI: Baker Academic, 2008), 107–24.

garden, but God said, 'You shall not eat of the fruit of the tree
that is in the midst of the garden, neither shall you touch it,
lest you die.'" (Gen. 3:1–3)

The snake does not begin by directly *contradicting* God. He begins by *questioning* God.

The snake craftily reframes the situation. Instead of emphasizing that Adam and Eve may eat from every tree except one, the snake asks whether they may eat from *any* tree.

Instead of rebuking the snake, the woman entertains the idea that God is not benevolent and trustworthy. Maybe God made up that rule to limit her pleasure. Her words "neither shall you touch it" may even embellish what God commanded.

The Snake Deceives by Contradicting God

But the serpent said to the woman, "*You will not surely die*. For
God knows that when you eat of it your eyes will be opened,
and you will be like God, knowing good and evil." (Gen. 3:4–5)

After the snake *questions* God, the snake intensifies his deceitful assault by *contradicting* God. He lies and blasphemes God as having selfish motives. This serpent sounds like the devil: "When he lies," explains Jesus, "he speaks out of his own character, for he is a liar and the father of lies" (John 8:44).

Yes, the woman's eyes will be opened, but not in a good way. She will know evil by becoming evil herself, and thus she will die spiritually. Little does she know in her innocence that this death will start the countdown to her physical death.

The Snake Deceives by Tempting with Worldliness

But the serpent said to the woman, "You will not surely die.
For God knows that when you eat of it your eyes will be

opened, and you will be like God, knowing good and evil." So when the woman saw that *the tree was good for food*, and that *it was a delight to the eyes*, and that *the tree was to be desired to make one wise* . . . (Gen. 3:4–6)

Worldliness is loving the world (see 1 John 2:15–17).[3] For us to "love the world" today (1 John 2:15) is to delight in the anti-God culture that permeates this fallen world, to take pleasure in worldly ways of thinking and acting, to take pleasure in what theologian John Frame calls "the bad part of culture."[4] Eve is the first human in history to love the world, and the snake deceives her by tempting her with worldliness—much as Satan later tempts Jesus in the wilderness (see table 2).

Table 2. Comparing Genesis 3:6, Luke 4:1–13, and 1 John 2:16

Genesis 3:6: The woman saw that . . .	Luke 4:1–13 (cf. Matt 4:1–11)	1 John 2:16
The tree was good for food.	Command this stone to become bread.	The desires of the flesh
It was a delight to the eyes.	If you, then, will worship me, it will all be yours.	The desires of the eyes
The tree was to be desired to make one wise.	If you are the Son of God, throw yourself down from here.	Pride of life

I am not certain that the three phrases in 1 John 2:16 line up exactly with Genesis 3:6 and Luke 4 or that John has these parallels in mind. But the three phrases in 1 John 2:16 seem to line up at least roughly with Genesis 3:6 and Luke 4, so the parallel seems legitimate.

---

3. Cf. Andrew David Naselli, "Do Not Love the World: Breaking the Evil Enchantment of Worldliness (A Sermon on 1 John 2:15–17)," *The Southern Baptist Journal of Theology* 22, no. 1 (2018): 111–25.

4. John M. Frame, *The Doctrine of the Christian Life*, A Theology of Lordship (Phillipsburg, NJ: P&R, 2008), 866. Cf. Albert M. Wolters, *Creation Regained: Biblical Basics for a Reformational Worldview*, 2nd ed. (Grand Rapids, MI: Eerdmans, 2005), 64: "*World* designates the totality of sin-infected creation. Wherever human sinfulness bends or twists or distorts God's good creation, there we find the 'world.'"

The three phrases in 1 John 2:16 are broad and overlapping ways to describe "all that is in the world":

1. "The desires of the flesh" are whatever your body sinfully craves. A person may crave forbidden food (like Eve did) or excessive food and drink or immoral sex or pornography or security in an idolatrous relationship. Our fundamental problem is not what is "out there" but what is "in here." It's not external but internal.

2. "The desires of the eyes" are whatever you sinfully crave when you see it. Basically, this craving is coveting—idolatrously wanting what you don't have.[5] My colleague Joe Rigney tells his sons that coveting is wanting something so bad that it makes you fussy. Eve idolatrously wanted what she didn't have.

3. "Pride of life" is arrogance produced by your material possessions or accomplishments. Consequently, you may strut around like a peacock, proudly displaying your fashionable clothes or latest gadget or social status. Or you may not be a peacock, yet you still find your security in your raw talents or achievements or savings account. You are proudly independent; you don't need God. In this case, Eve arrogantly wanted to be independent of God.

One Johannine scholar says of the three phrases in 1 John 2:16, "Translating this as 'sex, money, and power' may not miss the mark by much."[6]

---

5. John Piper, *Future Grace: The Purifying Power of the Promises of God*, in *The Collected Works of John Piper*, ed. David Mathis and Justin Taylor, vol. 4 (Wheaton, IL: Crossway, 2017), 241: "*Covetousness is desiring something so much that you lose your contentment in God.* . . . Coveting is desiring anything other than God in a way that betrays a loss of contentment and satisfaction in him. Covetousness is a heart divided between two gods. So Paul calls it idolatry." Compare the last sentence of 1 John: "Little children, keep yourselves from idols" (1 John 5:21).

6. D. Moody Smith, *First, Second, and Third John*, Interpretation: A Bible Commentary for Teaching and Preaching (Louisville: John Knox, 1991), 66. Cf. John Piper, *Living in the Light:*

The Snake Deceives Eve to Rebel against God, and Adam Follows Eve

> So when the woman saw that the tree was good for food, and that it was a delight to the eyes, and that the tree was to be desired to make one wise, *she took of its fruit and ate*, and *she also gave some to her husband who was with her, and he ate.* (Gen. 3:6)

> Then the LORD God said to the woman, "What is this that you have done?" The woman said, "*The serpent deceived me, and I ate.*" (Gen. 3:13)

> But I am afraid that as *the serpent deceived Eve by his cunning*, your thoughts will be led astray from a sincere and pure devotion to Christ. (2 Cor. 11:3)

> Adam was not deceived, but *the woman was deceived* and became a transgressor. (1 Tim. 2:14)

God commissioned his image bearers to rule over the beasts of the field (Gen. 1:26–27), but his image bearers committed treachery. Instead of obeying the King, they followed the snake.

Eve was not alone. Adam "was with her" (Gen. 3:6). So when Adam ate, he rebelled against God not only by failing to obey what God commanded but also by failing to lead and protect his wife. "Adam should have slain and thus judged the serpent in carrying out the mandate of Gen. 1:28 to 'rule and subdue,'" explains New Testament scholar G. K. Beale, but instead "the serpent ended up ruling over Adam and Eve by persuading them with deceptive words."[7]

Money, Sex, and Power; Making the Most of Three Dangerous Opportunities (Washington, DC: Good Book, 2016).

7. G. K. Beale, *A New Testament Biblical Theology: The Unfolding of the Old Testament in the New* (Grand Rapids, MI: Baker Academic, 2011), 34–35.

When God calls to "the man" and asks, "Where are you [singular]?" (Gen. 3:9), he directly addresses Adam—not both Adam and Eve. Adam is primarily responsible because he is the head of the husband-wife relationship. Thus, later Scripture blames Adam for the fall into sin (Rom. 5:12–21; 1 Cor. 15:21–22).[8] He should have killed the dragon and rescued the girl.

As a Result of the Snake's Deceit, Adam's and Eve's Sins Separate Them from God

> Then the eyes of both were opened, and they knew that they were naked. And they sewed fig leaves together and made themselves loincloths.
>
> And they heard the sound of the LORD God walking in the garden in the cool of the day, and *the man and his wife hid themselves from the presence of the LORD God* among the trees of the garden. But the LORD God called to the man and said to him, "Where are you?" And he said, "I heard the sound of you in the garden, and I was afraid, because I was naked, and I hid myself." He said, "Who told you that you were naked? Have you eaten of the tree of which I commanded you not to eat?" The man said, "The woman whom you gave to be with me, she gave me fruit of the tree, and I ate." Then the LORD God said to the woman, "What is this that you have done?" The woman said, "The serpent deceived me, and I ate." (Gen. 3:7–13)

Adam and Eve's nakedness symbolized their innocence (see Gen. 2:25), but after they sinned, they clothed themselves because they were no longer innocent (Gen. 3:6). They hid from God because they were ashamed to be in his presence (3:8). God gives Adam and

---

8. Cf. Raymond C. Ortlund Jr., "Male-Female Equality and Male Headship: Genesis 1–3," in *Recovering Biblical Manhood and Womanhood: A Response to Evangelical Feminism*, ed. John Piper and Wayne Grudem (Westchester, IL: Crossway, 1991), 107–8.

Eve the opportunity to confess their sins and take responsibility for them. But they justify themselves by making excuses: Adam blames Eve, and Eve blames the snake (3:12–13).

As a Result of the Snake's Deceit, God Curses the Snake and Promises a Snake Crusher

The LORD God said to the serpent,

> "Because you have done this,
>> *cursed are you* above all livestock
>> and above all beasts of the field;
> on your belly you shall go,
>> and dust you shall eat
>> all the days of your life.
> I will put enmity between you and the woman,
>> and between your offspring and her offspring;
> *he shall bruise your head*,
>> and you shall bruise his heel." (Gen. 3:14–15)

God may have originally created the snake with legs and wings—as in our popular picture of dragons. But because of the snake's deceit, God humiliated the snake by forcing it to slither on its belly in the dust. As a result, now we describe a snake as a reptile that is long, limbless, and without eyelids that moves over the ground on its belly with a flickering tongue, which makes the snake appear to be eating the dust.

God cursed not only the snake but also the snake's offspring. He cursed them with "enmity" (Gen. 3:15). The rest of the Bible's storyline traces the ongoing battle between the snake's offspring and the woman's offspring. The first seed of the serpent is Cain, who kills his brother Abel (Gen. 4:1–16). The serpent, Jesus explains, "was a murderer from the beginning" (John 8:44), and Cain was the first human murderer. Humans are either children of God or children of the devil (Matt. 13:38–39; John 8:33, 44; Acts 13:10; 1 John 3:8–10).

Instead of continuing through Abel, the seed of the woman continues through Seth: "God has appointed for me another offspring instead of Abel, for Cain killed him" (Gen. 4:25). That line continues through Noah (Gen. 6:9) and then through Abraham,[9] Isaac, Jacob, and Judah (Gen. 11–50) and eventually through David all the way to Jesus the Messiah and his followers.[10] The woman's offspring can refer to a group of people (the people of God collectively—cf. Rom. 16:20) and to a particular person (the Messiah—cf. Gal. 3:16).[11] Although the serpent will bruise the Messiah's heel (Jesus dies on a tree), Jesus is the ultimate seed of the woman who will mortally crush the serpent (cf. Gal. 3:16; Heb. 2:14–15; 1 John 3:8). "By going to the cross," explains New Testament scholar D. A. Carson, "Jesus will ultimately destroy this serpent, this devil, who holds people captive under sin, shame, and guilt. He will crush the serpent's head by taking their guilt and shame on himself."[12]

As a Result of the Snake's Deceit, God Punishes Eve and Adam

To the woman he said,

> "*I will surely multiply your pain in childbearing;*
> in pain you shall bring forth children.

---

9. See James M. Hamilton Jr., "The Seed of the Woman and the Blessing of Abraham," *Tyndale Bulletin* 58, no. 2 (2007): 253–73.

10. See John L. Ronning, "The Curse on the Serpent (Genesis 3:15) in Biblical Theology and Hermeneutics" (PhD diss., Westminster Theological Seminary, 1997); Michael Rydelnik, *The Messianic Hope: Is the Hebrew Bible Really Messianic?*, New American Commentary Studies in Bible and Theology 9 (Nashville: B&H, 2010), esp. 129–45.

11. See James M. Hamilton Jr., "The Skull Crushing Seed of the Woman: Inner-Biblical Interpretation of Genesis 3:15," *The Southern Baptist Journal of Theology* 10, no. 2 (2006): 30–55; Jason S. DeRouchie and Jason C. Meyer, "Christ or Family as the 'Seed' of Promise? An Evaluation of N. T. Wright on Galatians 3:16," *The Southern Baptist Journal of Theology* 14, no. 3 (2010): 36–48.

12. D. A. Carson, *The God Who Is There: Finding Your Place in God's Story* (Grand Rapids, MI: Baker, 2010), 37.

> *Your desire shall be contrary to your husband,*
>> but he shall rule over you."

And to Adam he said,

> "Because you have listened to the voice of your wife
>> and have eaten of the tree
> of which I commanded you,
>> 'You shall not eat of it,'
> *cursed is the ground because of you;*
>> in pain you shall eat of it all the days of your life;
> thorns and thistles it shall bring forth for you;
>> and you shall eat the plants of the field.
> By the sweat of your face
>> you shall eat bread,
> till you return to the ground,
>> for out of it you were taken;
> for you are dust,
>> and to dust you shall return." (Gen. 3:16–19)

God punished Eve and Adam with pain. He punished the woman with pain in childbearing[13] and with pain in how she and her husband struggle to lead in a marriage relationship. Instead of gladly following her husband, the woman desires either to dominate him by usurping his leadership or to possessively cling to him by wanting him to be more for her than he can. And instead of responsibly exer-

---

13. See Jesse R. Scheumann, "A Biblical Theology of Birth Pain and the Hope of the Messiah" (ThM thesis, Bethlehem College & Seminary, 2014). Scheumann concludes:

As paradoxical as it sounds, birth pain is a redemptive judgment. Judgment is the dominant connotation of the imagery throughout Scripture. But birth pain is redemptive in that the Messiah would come through the line of promise, through birth pain (Gen 3:15–16; 35:16–19; 38:27–29; Mic 4:9–10; 5:2–3[1–2]; Song 8:5; 1 Chr 4:9; Rev 12:2), and he would bear the judgment in birthing the new covenant people (Isa 42:14; Isa 53:10–12; John 16:20–22; Acts 2:24), just as God writhed in birthing creation (Ps 90:2; Prov 8:24–25) and in birthing the old covenant people (Deut 32:18). (115)

cising headship by lovingly leading his wife, the man selfishly fails to guide and protect his wife—either by treating his wife in a harsh and domineering manner (3:16) or by lazily abdicating primary leadership to his wife (3:1–6).

By cursing the ground, God punished the man with pain in cultivating the ground. Adam sinfully ate forbidden food; consequently, it is now more difficult to grow food. God created the earth as abundantly productive, but now he has cursed it.

Further, God punished mankind with mortality. As a result of physical death, humans return to the very ground over which the snake must now slither.

As a Result of the Snake's Deceit, God Clothes Adam and Eve with Garments of Skin

Then the eyes of both were opened, and they knew that they were naked. And they sewed fig leaves together and made themselves loincloths.

. . . But the LORD God called to the man and said to him, "Where are you?" And he said, "I heard the sound of you in the garden, and I was afraid, because I was naked, and I hid myself." He said, "Who told you that you were naked? Have you eaten of the tree of which I commanded you not to eat?" . . .

. . . And *the LORD God made for Adam and for his wife garments of skins and clothed them.* (Gen. 3:7, 9–11, 21)

Where did the garments of skin come from? God killed animals to cover the shame and guilt of their sin. This appears to anticipate animal sacrifice under the Mosaic law (cf. Lev. 1–7) and ultimately the substitutionary sacrifice of Jesus himself (cf. Rom. 3:21–26).

As a Result of the Snake's Deceit, God Banishes Adam and Eve from the Garden of Eden

> Then the LORD God said, "Behold, the man has become like one of us in knowing good and evil. Now, lest he reach out his hand and take also of the tree of life and eat, and live forever—" therefore *the LORD God sent him out from the garden of Eden* to work the ground from which he was taken. He drove out the man, and at the east of the garden of Eden *he placed the cherubim and a flaming sword that turned every way to guard the way to the tree of life.* (Gen. 3:22–24)

This part of the story connects to two major themes in the Bible's storyline.

1. *Exile and exodus.*[14] God banishes sinful people from his special presence (exile), and he redeems his people from exile (exodus). Here are some highlights of this theme that begin in Genesis 3: God exiles Cain to the land of Nod (Gen. 4), delivers Noah from the flood (Gen. 6–9), exiles rebellious people after the Tower of Babel (Gen. 11), brings Abraham out of Ur (Gen. 15), brings his people out of Egypt (Ex. 1–15), exiles the northern kingdom of Israel to Assyria (2 Kings 17) and the southern kingdom of Israel to Babylon (2 Kings 25), and delivers his people from exile in Assyria and Babylon back to the land. The climactic exile is Jesus's atoning death on the cross (Mark 15:34), and the climactic exodus is Jesus's resurrection. Now God's people have entered into rest (Heb. 3–4) while living as holy pilgrims in exile in this world (1 Pet. 1:17; 2:9–11). In the ultimate exodus, God's people

---

14. Cf. Iain M. Duguid, "Exile," in *New Dictionary of Biblical Theology*, ed. T. Desmond Alexander and Brian S. Rosner (Downers Grove, IL: InterVarsity Press, 2000), 475–78; Rikki E. Watts, "Exodus," in Alexander and Rosner, *New Dictionary of Biblical Theology*, 478–87; Thomas Richard Wood, "The Regathering of the People of God: An Investigation into the New Testament's Appropriation of the Old Testament Prophecies concerning the Regathering of Israel" (PhD diss., Trinity Evangelical Divinity School, 2006); Alastair J. Roberts and Andrew Wilson, *Echoes of Exodus: Tracing Themes of Redemption through Scripture* (Wheaton, IL: Crossway, 2018).

will forever enjoy God in the new heavens and new earth, and in the ultimate exile, God will forever banish his enemies from his presence.

2. *Temple*.[15] The temple theme begins with the garden of Eden. When God creates the heavens and the earth in Genesis 1–2, the garden of Eden is his dwelling place. God's dwelling place is associated with heaven, and he "comes down" to earth. The garden of Eden is the first temple, "the temple-garden," "a divine sanctuary."[16] It's the place where humans meet with God. There are many parallels between the garden of Eden and the tabernacle/temple. The Most Holy Place or the Holy of Holies in the tabernacle and temple kept the ark of the covenant surrounded by two elaborate, gold cherubim. This room was God's throne room, and only the high priest entered the Most Holy Place once a year to make atonement for the people. When priests served in the Holy Place, the inner veil kept them from seeing into the Most Holy Place.

God instructed the Israelites to skillfully weave cherubim into the inner veil (Ex. 26:31; cf. 36:35). The Most Holy Place parallels the garden of Eden. After God expelled Adam and Eve from the garden, "He drove out the man, and at the east of the garden of Eden he placed the cherubim and a flaming sword that turned every way to guard the way to the tree of life" (Gen. 3:24). In a similar way, the cherubim woven into the inner veil symbolized that sinful humans could not enter this temple either.

The temple theme climaxes in Jesus. Jesus, the God-man, "tabernacles" among humans. "The Word became flesh and dwelt [i.e., tabernacled] among us" (John 1:14). His body is the temple (John 2:18–22). And when he died on the cross, the veil between the Holy

---

15. See G. K. Beale, *The Temple and the Church's Mission: A Biblical Theology of the Dwelling Place of God*, New Studies in Biblical Theology 17 (Downers Grove, IL: InterVarsity Press, 2004); G. K. Beale and Mitchell Kim, *God Dwells among Us: Expanding Eden to the Ends of the Earth* (Downers Grove, IL: InterVarsity Press, 2014).

16. T. Desmond Alexander, *From Eden to the New Jerusalem: An Introduction to Biblical Theology* (Grand Rapids, MI: Kregel, 2008), 20–21.

Place and the Most Holy Place "was torn in two, from top to bottom" (Matt. 27:51). Jesus's death makes it possible for people to go directly into God's presence (see Heb. 6:19–20; 10:19–22). The temple rituals and the Mosaic law-covenant are now obsolete. Jesus is our temple, our priest, our sacrifice.[17]

Now the church is collectively God's temple (1 Cor. 3:16–17; 2 Cor. 6:14–7:1; Eph. 2:21–22; 1 Pet. 2:4–10). So is the individual Christian's body (1 Cor. 6:19–20). The ultimate temple is the new Jerusalem (Rev. 21). "And I saw no temple in the city, for its temple is the Lord God the Almighty and the Lamb" (Rev. 21:22).

The Snake Is Satan

> I want you to be wise as to what is good and innocent as to what is evil [cf. Gen. 3:5]. The God of peace will soon *crush Satan* under your feet. (Rom. 16:19–20)

> But I am afraid that as the *serpent* deceived Eve by his cunning, your thoughts will be led astray from a sincere and pure devotion to Christ. (2 Cor. 11:3)

> And another sign appeared in heaven: behold, a *great red dragon*, with seven heads and ten horns, and on his heads seven diadems.
>
> And the *great dragon* was thrown down, that *ancient serpent*, who is called the *devil* and *Satan*, the *deceiver* of the whole world—he was thrown down to the earth, and his angels were thrown down with him. . . . "The *accuser of our brothers* has been thrown down, who accuses them day and night before our God. . . . The *devil* has come down to you in great wrath, because he knows that his time is short!" (Rev. 12:3, 9, 10, 12)

---

17. See Timothy Keller, *King's Cross: The Story of the World in the Life of Jesus* (New York: Dutton, 2011), 48.

> And he seized the *dragon*, that *ancient serpent*, who is the *devil* and *Satan*, and bound him for a thousand years. (Rev. 20:2)

Many commentators on Genesis 3 highlight that the text does not explicitly identify the snake as Satan. Some concede that the New Testament identifies the snake as Satan yet are reluctant to interpret Genesis 3 in that way.[18] Some insist that the snake in Genesis 3 is *not* Satan but instead embodies life, wisdom, and chaos.[19] But when we read Genesis 3 in light of the whole Bible, we must identify the snake as Satan.[20]

The Bible does not specify the precise way Satan and the snake in the garden of Eden relate, but Satan somehow used the physical body of a snake in Eden. He may have transformed himself into a snake-like creature, or he may have entered and influenced one of the existing snakes to accomplish his devious plan. Regardless of the precise means, the Bible presents the story of the talking snake as real history—not as a myth or legend or fable (and the Bible presents Adam and Eve as really existing as the first human beings in history).[21]

Transition: The Serpent after Genesis 3

At the story's beginning, the Bible teaches that the snake is deceitful. As the story progresses, the serpent's strategy alternates between deceiving as a snake and devouring as a dragon.

18. E.g., John H. Walton, *Genesis*, NIV Application Commentary (Grand Rapids, MI: Zondervan, 2001), 210; Walton, *The Lost World of Adam and Eve: Genesis 2–3 and the Human Origins Debate* (Downers Grove, IL: InterVarsity Press, 2015), 128–39.

19. E.g., Karen Randolph Joines, *Serpent Symbolism in the Old Testament: A Linguistic, Archaeological, and Literary Study* (Haddonfield, NJ: Haddonfield, 1974), 16–41, esp. 26–27.

20. Cf. Kenneth A. Mathews, *Genesis 1–11:26*, New American Commentary 1A (Nashville: Broadman & Holman, 1996), 234–35.

21. See James K. Hoffmeier, "Genesis 1–11 as History and Theology," in *Genesis: History, Fiction, or Neither? Three Views on the Bible's Earliest Chapters*, ed. Charles Halton, Counterpoints (Grand Rapids, MI: Zondervan, 2015), 23–58 (also 98–100, 140–49); Wayne Grudem, "Theistic Evolution Undermines Twelve Creation Events and Several Crucial Christian Doctrines," in *Theistic Evolution: A Scientific, Philosophical, and Theological Critique*, ed. J. P. Moreland et al. (Wheaton, IL: Crossway, 2017), 783–837; Vern S. Poythress, *Interpreting Eden: A Guide to Faithfully Reading and Understanding Genesis 1–3* (Wheaton, IL: Crossway, 2019).

2

Snakes and Dragons between the Bible's Bookends—Part 1

The Good, the Bad, and the Ultimate Serpent

A symbol does not have to represent only good or only evil. A lion can symbolize Jesus (Rev. 5:5) or Satan (1 Pet. 5:8). Leaven can symbolize how the kingdom of God spreads (Matt. 13:33) or how evil spreads (1 Cor. 5:6–8). And serpents can symbolize either good or evil.

Serpents Occasionally Symbolize Good

Most people think that serpent symbolism is intrinsically negative—such as the Slytherin House or the snake Nagini in *Harry Potter*. But serpent symbolism can be positive. For example, a serpent is prominent in the symbol for emergency medical services in many countries. In the United States, that symbol appears on ambulances. The logo is called the Star of Life, and it features a snake wrapped around the staff of Asclepius, a Greek god associated with healing and medicine.

Though not often, serpents sometimes symbolize good rather than evil in the Bible. The first reference to serpents in the Bible is positive: "God created the great sea creatures [Heb. *tannin*]" (Gen. 1:21). In Canaanite creation myths, the gods had to defeat the already existing sea monsters before they could create the world, but in actual history God created the sea monsters.[1] Great serpents demonstrate God's creative power—something psalmists praise God for:

O Lord, how manifold are your works!
> In wisdom have you made them all;
> the earth is full of your creatures.
Here is the sea, great and wide,
> which teems with creatures innumerable,
> living things both small and great.
There go the ships,
> and *Leviathan*, which you formed to play in it.
>> (Ps. 104:24–26)

Praise the Lord from the earth,
> you *great sea creatures* and all deeps,
fire and hail, snow and mist,
> stormy wind fulfilling his word! (Ps. 148:7–8)

Some scholars even speculate that the seraphim in Isaiah 6:2–3 are winged serpents, because other passages apply the same term to

---

1. Cf. Kenneth A. Kitchen, "Serpent," in *New Bible Dictionary*, ed. I. Howard Marshall et al., 3rd ed. (Downers Grove, IL: InterVarsity Press, 1996), 1081; John D. Currid, *Against the Gods: The Polemical Theology of the Old Testament* (Wheaton, IL: Crossway, 2013), 44–45. In contrast, some biblical scholars approach the dragon in the Bible as a parallel to other cultures and thus view the dragon as a myth—for example, Robert D. Miller II, *The Dragon, the Mountain, and the Nations: An Old Testament Myth, Its Origins, and Its Afterlives*, Explorations in Ancient Near Eastern Civilizations 6 (University Park, PA: Eisenbrauns, 2016).

fiery serpents (Num. 21:6; Deut. 8:15; Isa. 14:29; 30:6).[2] It's possible that seraphim look like holy dragons, but I think it's more likely that *seraphim* simply means *fiery ones* and that other passages apply that term to serpents because their poisonous bites feel like a fiery burn.

When Jacob blesses his sons, he says this about Dan:

> Dan shall be a serpent in the way,
>> a viper by the path,
> that bites the horse's heels
>> so that his rider falls backward. (Gen. 49:17)

A serpent (a small animal) can terrify a horse (a large animal) with shrewd skill (cf. Amos 9:3). Similarly, Dan (a small tribe) will defeat disproportionately larger enemies with shrewd skill (e.g., Judg. 18:7–10, 27).

A proverb marvels at the mesmerizing "way of a serpent on a rock" (Prov. 30:19). And Jesus tells his disciples, "I am sending you out as sheep in the midst of wolves, so be wise as serpents and innocent as doves" (Matt. 10:16). To describe serpents as shrewd focuses on a positive quality.[3]

Serpents Usually Symbolize Evil

But serpents are overwhelmingly negative in the Bible. For God's people under the old covenant, serpents were unclean (Lev. 11:41–43). Throughout the Bible, serpents most commonly symbolize what is dangerous because they are proverbially poisonous

---

2. E.g., Karen Randolph Joines, *Serpent Symbolism in the Old Testament: A Linguistic, Archaeological, and Literary Study* (Haddonfield, NJ: Haddonfield, 1974), 42–60.

3. As Jesus's disciples face dangerous situations, explains Eckhard J. Schnabel, "They should be 'wise as serpents'; that is, they should behave circumspectly, prudently, carefully considering the dangers, so that their reliance on God's protection becomes evident. They must neither seek martyrdom nor play evasive or tactical games: they must be 'innocent as doves'—that is, not cunning, overcautious, suspicious of everybody and everything. Jesus warns them against both foolhardy confidence and calculating furtiveness." Eckhard J. Schnabel, *Early Christian Mission*, 2 vols. (Downers Grove, IL: InterVarsity Press, 2004), 1:300–301.

and deadly. The Bible frequently associates serpents with deadly venom and poison:

> Though evil is sweet in his mouth,
> > though he hides it under his tongue,
> though he is loath to let it go
> > and holds it in his mouth,
> yet his food is turned in his stomach;
> > it is *the venom of cobras* within him.
> He swallows down riches and vomits them up again;
> > God casts them out of his belly.
> He will suck *the poison of cobras*;
> > *the tongue of a viper will kill him.* (Job 20:12–16)

> The wicked are estranged from the womb;
> > they go astray from birth, speaking lies.
> They have *venom like the venom of a serpent,*
> > like the deaf *adder* that stops its ear,
> so that it does not hear the voice of charmers
> > or of the cunning enchanter. (Ps. 58:3–5)

> They make their tongue *sharp as a serpent's,*
> > and under their lips is *the venom of asps.* (Ps. 140:3,
> > > which Paul quotes in Rom. 3:13)

Serpents are dangerous because their bite injects poison into their victims. Wine "bites like a serpent and stings like an adder" (Prov. 23:32). A serpent's bite illustrates misfortunes (see Eccles. 10:8–11; Amos 5:18–19).

One metaphor portrays sinners hatching the eggs of an adder (Isa. 59:5). The eggs of a *robin* wouldn't be as sinister. Isaiah comments about those sinister eggs,

He who eats their eggs dies,
> and from one that is crushed *a viper is hatched*. (Isa. 59:5)

Bible stories that mention serpents typically assume that serpents are deadly and fear-inducing.

> Or which one of you, if his son asks him for bread, will give him a stone? Or if he asks for a fish, will give him *a serpent*? If you then, who are evil, know how to give good gifts to your children, how much more will your Father who is in heaven give good things to those who ask him! (Matt. 7:9–11; cf. Luke 11:11–13)

Ancient people didn't know the precise mechanisms by which snake venom worked, but they were well aware of its effects. When a viper came out of a bundle of sticks and fastened on Paul's hand, the natives of Malta "were waiting for him to swell up or suddenly fall down dead." When he didn't, they concluded that "he was a god" (Acts 28:3–6).

The sixth-trumpet judgment in Revelation includes beings whose "tails are like serpents with heads, and by means of them they wound" (Rev. 9:19). Serpents in the Bible usually symbolize evil.

Serpents Distinctly Symbolize God's Enemies— Satan and His Offspring

Starting with Genesis 3, the Bible connects the serpent to sin and the curse. More specifically, serpents symbolize God's enemies. The following four passages equate serpents with the enemy of God and his people:

> For their rock is not as our Rock;
> > *our enemies* are by themselves.
> For their vine comes from the vine of Sodom
> > and from the fields of Gomorrah;

their grapes are grapes of poison;
> their clusters are bitter;

their wine is the poison of serpents
> *and the cruel venom of asps.* (Deut. 32:31–33)

For he will command his angels concerning you
> *to guard you* in all your ways.

On their hands they will bear you up,
> lest you strike your foot against a stone.

You will tread on the lion and *the adder*;
> the young lion and *the serpent you will trample*
> > *underfoot.* (Ps. 91:11–13)

The nations shall see and be ashamed of all their might;
they shall lay their hands on their mouths;
> their ears shall be deaf;

they shall lick the dust like a serpent [cf. Gen. 3:14],
> *like the crawling things of the earth*;

they shall come trembling out of their strongholds;
> they shall turn in dread to the LORD our God,
> and they shall be in fear of you. (Mic. 7:16–17)

The seventy-two returned with joy, saying, "Lord, even the demons are subject to us in your name!" And he said to them, "I saw Satan fall like lightning from heaven. Behold, *I have given you authority to tread on serpents* and scorpions, and *over all the power of the enemy*, and nothing shall hurt you." (Luke 10:17–19)

The Ultimate Serpent Is Satan

Satan is the ultimate serpent. He is *the* serpent that energizes other serpents to craftily deceive and devour people. And he will ultimately fail: "In that day the LORD with his hard and great and strong sword will punish Leviathan the fleeing serpent, Leviathan the twisting serpent, and he will slay the dragon that is in the sea" (Isa. 27:1).

SATAN TEMPTS GOD'S PEOPLE

Satan is the most crafty snake. His strategy is to deceive, tempt, lie, and backstab. His primary prey is God's people. And he is so arrogant and self-deceived that he tried to tempt Jesus!

> Jesus was led up by the Spirit into the wilderness to be *tempted by the devil*. And after fasting forty days and forty nights, he was hungry. And *the tempter* came and said to him, "If you are the Son of God, command these stones to become loaves of bread." (Matt. 4:1–3; cf. Luke 4:2)

Satan so routinely tempts God's people that the Bible gives him the title "the tempter" (Matt. 4:3; 1 Thess. 3:5). Tempting God's people is what Satan does: "Do not deprive one another, except perhaps by agreement for a limited time, that you may devote yourselves to prayer; but then come together again, *so that Satan may not tempt you* because of your lack of self-control" (1 Cor. 7:5). Many Christians in the modern Western world seem embarrassed to treat Satan as a personal being. But Paul ascribes one of the most common temptations in life at least in part to the personal agency of Satan.

Satan deceitfully schemes to outwit God's people. That's why God's people must "stand against the schemes of the devil" (Eph. 6:11).

> Anyone whom you forgive, I also forgive. Indeed, what I have forgiven, if I have forgiven anything, has been for your sake in the presence of Christ, *so that we would not be outwitted by Satan*; for we are not ignorant of *his designs*. (2 Cor. 2:10–11)

> For such men are false apostles, deceitful workmen, disguising themselves as apostles of Christ. And no wonder, for *even Satan disguises himself as an angel of light.* So it is no surprise if his servants, also, disguise themselves as servants of righteousness. Their end will correspond to their deeds. (2 Cor. 11:13–15)

> For this reason, when I could bear it no longer, I sent to learn about your faith, for fear that somehow *the tempter had tempted you* and our labor would be in vain. (1 Thess. 3:5)

> The coming of the lawless one is by *the activity of Satan with all power and false signs and wonders, and with all wicked deception* for those who are perishing, because they refused to love the truth and so be saved. (2 Thess. 2:9–10)

> And the Lord's servant must not be quarrelsome but kind to everyone, able to teach, patiently enduring evil, correcting his opponents with gentleness. God may perhaps grant them repentance leading to a knowledge of the truth, and they may come to their senses and escape from *the snare of the devil, after being captured by him to do his will.* (2 Tim. 2:24–26)

Tempting people is satanic. It's serpentine. God does not tempt people.

> Let no one say when he is tempted, "I am being tempted by God," for God cannot be tempted with evil, and *he himself tempts no one.* But *each person is tempted when he is lured and enticed by his own desire.* Then desire when it has conceived gives birth to sin, and sin when it is fully grown brings forth death.
>
> Do not be deceived, my beloved brothers. (James 1:13–16)

Satan is the ultimate deceptive snake. He hates God, and he hates God's people. He does everything he can to harm God's people, and one of his primary strategies is to tempt God's people to desire what God forbids and thus to believe what is not true and to do what is not right.

JESUS HELPS HIS PEOPLE WHEN SATAN TEMPTS THEM

Satan, the deceptive snake, is a deadly, fear-inducing enemy. But here's why God's people should not despair that the snake tempts them:

> Since therefore the children share in flesh and blood, he [i.e., Jesus] himself likewise partook of the same things, that *through death he might destroy the one who has the power of death, that is, the devil, and deliver all those who through fear of death were subject to lifelong slavery.* For surely it is not angels that he helps, but *he helps the offspring of Abraham.* Therefore he had to be made like his brothers in every respect, so that he might become *a merciful and faithful high priest* in the service of God, to make propitiation for the sins of the people. For *because he himself has suffered when tempted, he is able to help those who are being tempted.* (Heb. 2:14–18)

> Since then *we have a great high priest* who has passed through the heavens, Jesus, the Son of God, let us hold fast our confession. For *we do not have a high priest who is unable to sympathize* [NIV: "empathize"] *with our weaknesses, but one who in every respect has been tempted as we are, yet without sin.* Let us then with confidence draw near to the throne of grace, that *we may receive mercy and find grace to help in time of need.* (Heb. 4:14–16)

Jesus became human to decisively defeat the snake and save his people. Thus, Jesus can help his people when Satan tempts them. Jesus is a merciful and faithful high priest who empathizes with his people.

God Is Sovereign over Leviathan

The book of Job refers several times to a monster sea serpent called Leviathan or Rahab:

> Let those curse it who curse the day,
>> who are ready to rouse up *Leviathan*. (Job 3:8)

God is sovereign over this serpent.

> God will not turn back his anger;
>> beneath him bowed the helpers of *Rahab* [NLT: "Even
>>> the *monsters of the sea* are crushed beneath his feet."]
>> (Job 9:13)

> By his power he stilled the sea;
>> by his understanding he shattered *Rahab*.
> By his wind the heavens were made fair;
>> his hand pierced *the fleeing serpent*.
> Behold, these are but the outskirts of his ways,
>> and how small a whisper do we hear of him!
>> But the thunder of his power who can understand?
>> (Job 26:12–14)

When God interrogates and rebukes Job, he describes Leviathan in detail to emphasize that he is supremely sovereign over the mighty creature. Job 41 is the longest passage in the Bible about a monstrous serpent:

> Can you draw out *Leviathan* with a fishhook
>> or press down his tongue with a cord?
> Can you put a rope in his nose
>> or pierce his jaw with a hook?
> Will he make many pleas to you?
>> Will he speak to you soft words?

Will he make a covenant with you
    to take him for your servant forever?
Will you play with him as with a bird,
    or will you put him on a leash for your girls?
Will traders bargain over him?
    Will they divide him up among the merchants?
Can you fill his skin with harpoons
    or his head with fishing spears?
Lay your hands on him;
    remember the battle—you will not do it again!
Behold, the hope of a man is false;
    he is laid low even at the sight of him.
No one is so fierce that he dares to stir him up.
    Who then is he who can stand before me?
Who has first given to me, that I should repay him?
    Whatever is under the whole heaven is mine.

I will not keep silence concerning his limbs,
    or his mighty strength, or his goodly frame.
Who can strip off his outer garment?
    Who would come near him with a bridle?
Who can open the doors of his face?
    Around his teeth is terror.
His back is made of rows of shields,
    shut up closely as with a seal.
One is so near to another
    that no air can come between them.
They are joined one to another;
    they clasp each other and cannot be separated.
His sneezings flash forth light,
    and his eyes are like the eyelids of the dawn.

Out of his mouth go flaming torches;
>   sparks of fire leap forth.
Out of his nostrils comes forth smoke,
>   as from a boiling pot and burning rushes.
His breath kindles coals,
>   and a flame comes forth from his mouth.
In his neck abides strength,
>   and terror dances before him.
The folds of his flesh stick together,
>   firmly cast on him and immovable.
His heart is hard as a stone,
>   hard as the lower millstone.
When he raises himself up, the mighty are afraid;
>   at the crashing they are beside themselves.
Though the sword reaches him, it does not avail,
>   nor the spear, the dart, or the javelin.
He counts iron as straw,
>   and bronze as rotten wood.
The arrow cannot make him flee;
>   for him, sling stones are turned to stubble.
Clubs are counted as stubble;
>   he laughs at the rattle of javelins.
His underparts are like sharp potsherds;
>   he spreads himself like a threshing sledge on the mire.
He makes the deep boil like a pot;
>   he makes the sea like a pot of ointment.
Behind him he leaves a shining wake;
>   one would think the deep to be white-haired.
On earth there is not his like,
>   a creature without fear.

He sees everything that is high;

he is king over all the sons of pride. (41:1–34)

The literary context of Job 41 is significant. Before God interrogates Job in chapters 40–41, Job steadfastly maintains that he is innocent in his suffering—and rightly so.[4] But Job is wrong in at least two ways:

1. Job concludes that *God is unjust* for allowing his innocent suffering (cf. 27:2–6).
2. Job presumes that *God owes him an explanation*. He repeatedly wishes to appeal directly to God and get a hearing with him (13:13–23; 23:3–9; 31:35–37; cf. 9:32–33).

All will be well, Job thinks, if only he can interview God. But when Job finally gets his wish to speak with God, the interview is not what he had in mind. God responds to Job but not on Job's terms; God responds on his own terms. Job doesn't question God; God questions Job. And God does so by thundering out of the whirlwind (38:1; 40:6).

The exchange between God and Job (38:1–42:6) reveals that in Job's eyes (1) God is too small and (2) Job is too large. God is not obligated to give Job anything—not even answers to his questions. So God changes the subject. That's why a Christian journalist humorously summarizes the book of Job like this:

Job in a nutshell:

Job: Why?

Friends: You sinned.

Job: No I didn't.

God: Look at the cool animals![5]

---

4. This section condenses and updates Andrew David Naselli, *From Typology to Doxology: Paul's Use of Isaiah and Job in Romans 11:34–35* (Eugene, OR: Pickwick, 2012), 63–90.

5. Ted Olsen (@tedolsen), Twitter, August 12, 2011, 6:21 a.m., https://twitter.com/tedolsen /status/102006913314734080.

God does not answer Job's main question: "Why am I suffering?" The closest God comes to answering it is rebuking Job for defending his own righteousness at the expense of God's righteousness (40:8).

When God interrogates Job in round one (38:2–40:2), God asks Job a series of stunning, humbling questions about creation. God's point is that only he controls every aspect of his creation and that Job cannot control any of them.

When God interrogates Job in round two (40:6–41:34), God asks Job a series of stunning, humbling questions about Behemoth (40:15–24) and Leviathan (41:1–34). There are at least three major views on how to identify Behemoth and Leviathan:

1. They are physical animals (e.g., dinosaurs or the hippopotamus and crocodile).
2. They are mythological creatures that represent evil, primordial, cosmic, chaotic forces.
3. They are physical animals (view 1) that also symbolize evil cosmic forces (view 2).

I find view 3 most compelling. The evidence for evil cosmic forces (view 2) is too strong to dismiss,[6] but Behemoth and Levia-

---

6. See the other four references to Leviathan: Job 3:8; Pss. 74:14; 104:26; Isa. 27:1. Cf. Christopher Ash, *Job: The Wisdom of the Cross*, Preaching the Word (Wheaton, IL: Crossway, 2014), 423; René A. López, "The Meaning of 'Behemoth' and 'Leviathan' in Job," *Bibliotheca Sacra* 173, no. 692 (2016): 401–24; Sidney Greidanus, *From Chaos to Cosmos: Creation to New Creation*, Short Studies in Biblical Theology (Wheaton, IL: Crossway, 2018), 60–63. For a compelling argument that Behemoth represents death and that Leviathan represents Satan, see Robert S. Fyall, *Now My Eyes Have Seen You: Images of Creation and Evil in the Book of Job*, New Studies in Biblical Theology 12 (Downers Grove, IL: InterVarsity Press, 2002), 101–74. Some adherents of view 2 prefer not to use the ambiguous word *mythological* since that might imply that the creatures are fictional or untrue. Cf. Ash, *Job*, 420:

Behemoth and Leviathan are storybook creatures, but they are also utterly real and true; it is just that their truth is conveyed to us in storybook descriptions that arouse in us a response of visceral fear. In this way they convey to us the truth of Satan much more powerfully than a calm and measured theological description would do. To a generation more familiar with the Harry Potter stories, we might want to compare Satan to Voldemort. We are therefore on strong Biblical ground when we identify the Leviathan at the end of the book of Job with the Satan at the start. This also answers a popular objection to the integ-

than also seem to be earthly creatures, because God tells Job that he created Behemoth (and, by implication, Leviathan) just as he created Job (40:15).

Whether you hold to any of those three views, you should be able to agree on why it is significant that God mentions Behemoth and Leviathan: *God created these powerful, fear-inducing creatures, and only God can control them.* God is God; Job is not. Therefore, Job's respectful fear of God should surpass his respectful fear of Behemoth and Leviathan.

If view 2 or 3 is correct, then Job 41 not only teaches that God controls the *earthly* dimensions of Job's suffering; it also teaches that God controls the *cosmic* ones—namely, Satan himself. God is more powerful than Satan. And that is exactly what the book of Job teaches:

- When Satan joins the sons of God (apparently God's angels) as they present themselves before God, *God initiates* a discussion with Satan about Job (1:6–8). Satan accuses Job of serving God merely because God has blessed Job, and *God gives Satan permission* to test Job but not touch him (1:9–12).

- Again Satan joins God's angels as they present themselves before God, and *again God initiates* a discussion with Satan about Job (2:1–3). Satan accuses Job of serving God merely because God has blessed him with health, and *God gives Satan permission* to touch Job but not kill him (2:4–6).

- God allows Satan to afflict Job, but *he does not merely allow it.* The epilogue describes Job's Satan-inflicted calamities as "all the evil that the LORD had brought upon him" (42:11). This is consistent with the prologue, where

---

rity of the book, namely, that the Satan plays a critical role at the start and then disappears from view. He does not disappear from view; he appears in all his evil terror at the end.

> God twice initiates discussions with Satan about Job (1:8;
> 2:3). The end of God's statement in 2:3—"you incited me
> [i.e., God] against him to destroy him without reason"—
> implies that *God himself is the ultimate cause of the calam-*
> *ity* since he, not Satan, is the one who destroys Job.

God is sovereign over serpents, which often symbolize God's enemies. And God's enemies ultimately do what God decrees. For example, when Amos prophesies that God will judge Israel, the Lord says,

> If they hide themselves on the top of Carmel,
>   from there I will search them out and take them;
> and if they hide from my sight at the bottom of the sea,
>   there *I will command the serpent*, and it shall bite them.
>   (Amos 9:3)

The serpent is out to kill and destroy God's image bearers, but
God is sovereign over the serpent. God is more powerful than Levia-
than. God is sovereign over Satan (cf. 2 Cor. 12:7–10). Christopher
Ash expresses how that should move God's people to respond:

> Evil frightens me. It is meant to. I am meant to be humbled by
> supernatural evil so that I know—deeply know—that it is too
> strong for me, that I cannot resist it on my own. Death and the
> one who holds the power of death—that is, the devil—are too
> strong for me. But my response is not meant to end in terror.
> For at the climax of the book of Job is this assurance that both
> death (the Behemoth) and the one who holds the power of
> death (the Leviathan) are creatures entirely under the control
> of the Sovereign God who is my Savior. . . .
>   The most evil deed in the history of the human race, the
> moment when the Leviathan and the Behemoth seemed ulti-

mately victorious, was the moment that was brought about by "the definite plan and foreknowledge of God" (Acts 2:23), and that was the moment of the Behemoth's and the Leviathan's definitive defeat. This God who knows how to use supernatural evil to serve his purposes of ultimate good can and will use the darkest invasions into my own life for his definite and invincible plans for my good in Christ. Hallelujah! What a Savior![7]

GOD WILL SLAY THE DRAGON

In that day *the LORD with his hard and great and strong sword will punish Leviathan the fleeing serpent, Leviathan the twisting serpent*, and *he will slay the dragon that is in the sea*. (Isa. 27:1)

Isaiah 27:1 describes the Lord's sword with three adjectives (hard, great, and strong), and it also describes the serpent in three ways (Leviathan the fleeing serpent, Leviathan the twisting serpent, and the dragon that is in the sea). Isaiah characterizes Leviathan in a way that complements how the book of Job appropriates it. Isaiah is not adopting a pagan mythological worldview—such as the Babylonian myth that the god Marduk had to defeat the dragon Tiamat in order to create the world. Instead, Isaiah is using a well-known concept in the ancient Near East to describe what is actually true—namely, that God will sovereignly destroy the most powerful evil monster in the universe.[8] The book of Revelation identifies this ancient serpent-monster as Satan (see chap. 4 below). And Paul promises, "The God of peace will soon crush Satan under your feet" (Rom. 16:20).

---

7. Ash, *Job*, 423–24.

8. Cf. John N. Oswalt, *The Book of Isaiah: Chapters 1–39*, The New International Commentary on the Old Testament (Grand Rapids, MI: Eerdmans, 1986), 490–91; Oswalt, *The Bible among the Myths: Unique Revelation or Just Ancient Literature?* (Grand Rapids, MI: Zondervan, 2009), 93–96; John N. Day, "God and Leviathan in Isaiah 27:1," *Bibliotheca Sacra* 155, no. 620 (1998): 423–36; J. Alec Motyer, *The Prophecy of Isaiah: An Introduction and Commentary* (Downers Grove, IL: InterVarsity Press, 1993), 408.

Consequently, Serpents Will No Longer Be Deadly

The Messiah, the "shoot from the stump of Jesse," will "kill the wicked" (Isa. 11:1, 4). As a result,

> The wolf shall dwell with the lamb,
>> and the leopard shall lie down with the young goat,
> and the calf and the lion and the fattened calf together;
>> and a little child shall lead them.
> The cow and the bear shall graze;
>> their young shall lie down together;
>> and the lion shall eat straw like the ox.
> *The nursing child shall play over the hole of the cobra,*
>> *and the weaned child shall put his hand on the*
>>> *adder's den.*
> *They shall not hurt or destroy*
>> *in all my holy mountain;*
> for the earth shall be full of the knowledge of the LORD
>> as the waters cover the sea. (Isa. 11:6–9)

> For behold, I create *new heavens*
>> *and a new earth,*
> and the former things shall not be remembered
>> or come into mind. . . .
> The wolf and the lamb shall graze together;
>> the lion shall eat straw like the ox,
>> and *dust shall be the serpent's food* [cf. Gen. 3:14].
> *They shall not hurt or destroy*
>> *in all my holy mountain* [repeats Isa. 11:9a],
>>> says the LORD. (Isa. 65:17, 25)

As a result of God's slaying *the* serpent in the future, serpents will no longer be deadly to humans. God will defang the serpent. Poisonous serpents are currently deadly, but God will transform them so that they become harmless. Even helpless toddlers will be able to play with serpents without danger. Serpents will no longer harm people. God's people will be safe and secure.

It's possible that the deadly animals in these passages refer exclusively to actual animals. In other words, when God transforms the earth, he will reverse the curse of Genesis 3:17–18 with the result that dangerous animals will no longer be dangerous (cf. Rom. 8:19–22). That may be the case, but it's more likely that the deadly animals in these passages metaphorically symbolize anything that makes God's people feel unsafe and insecure (including poisonous serpents). In other words, in this fallen world all sorts of predators may terrorize God's people (whether actual animals or people who oppose God and his people), but when God creates the new heaven and earth (Isa. 65:17), he will remove all dangerous creatures, with the result that they can no longer harm God's people (cf. Isa. 2:4). The basis for such bliss is that

> the earth shall be full of the knowledge of the LORD
> as the waters cover the sea. (Isa. 11:9)[9]

Isaiah 65:25 condenses 11:6–9, but it also adds that "dust shall be the serpent's food." This addition alludes to God's cursing the serpent in Genesis 3:14, and it points to God's ultimately defeating *the serpent* in Revelation 12 and 20 (see chap. 4 below).

Conclusion

It's rare for snakes to symbolize good in the Bible. They usually symbolize what is evil—what is poisonous and deadly. Satan is the ultimate serpent. The next chapter explores how the Bible depicts Satan's offspring as serpents.

---

9. Cf. G. K. Beale, "An Amillennial Response to a Premillennial View of Isaiah 65:20," *Journal of the Evangelical Theological Society* 61, no. 3 (2018): 461–92. On the millennium, see the discussion in chap. 4 below.

3

Snakes and Dragons between the Bible's Bookends—Part 2

Six Offspring of the Serpent

Satan—the ultimate serpent—has evil offspring. He energizes his offspring to be serpents that craftily deceive and devour people. The Bible depicts at least six categories of the serpent's offspring: (1) Egypt and its Pharaoh, (2) wicked leaders in Canaan and Moab, (3) the king of Babylon, (4) King Herod, (5) Pharisees and Sadducees, and (6) other false teachers.

Egypt and Its Pharaoh: A Dragon in the Seas

The Lord tells Pharaoh, king of Egypt, "you are like a dragon in the seas" (Ezek. 32:2). Egypt—specifically Pharaoh—is a serpent. Egypt is a snake, a Leviathan, a sea monster, a dragon in the seas. This is explicit in Exodus, Numbers, Psalms, Isaiah, and Ezekiel.

THE DRAGON MURDERS BABIES

The serpent hates the woman's offspring (Gen. 3:15). One of the serpent's strategies to fight the woman's offspring is to be a devouring dragon that murders babies. This happens with Pharaoh (Ex. 1:8–22), and the trajectory continues with King Herod (Matt. 2:16–18) and the dragon in the book of Revelation (Rev. 12:1–5).

> Then the king of Egypt said to the Hebrew midwives, one of whom was named Shiphrah and the other Puah, "When you serve as midwife to the Hebrew women and see them on the birthstool, *if it is a son, you shall kill him*, but if it is a daughter, she shall live." . . . Then Pharaoh commanded all his people, "*Every son that is born to the Hebrews you shall cast into the Nile*, but you shall let every daughter live." (Ex. 1:15–16, 22)

The dragon hates babies—humans made in God's image, humans who may be the woman's promised offspring. The devouring dragon *murders* babies.[1]

GOD DELIVERS HIS PEOPLE FROM THE EGYPTIAN SERPENT IN THE EXODUS

A new pharaoh who didn't know Joseph ruthlessly enslaved and oppressed the Israelites (Ex. 1). God commissioned Moses to liberate his people.

As God prepared Moses to face Pharaoh, God told Moses to throw his staff on the ground. When Moses did that, his staff "became *a serpent*, and Moses ran from it. But the LORD said to Moses, 'Put out your hand and catch it by the tail'—so he put out

---

1. The *son* language is significant because God calls his people his "firstborn son" (Ex. 4:22) and threatens to kill the firstborn sons in Egypt if Pharaoh will not let his people go (Ex. 4:23; cf. 12:29–30).

his hand and caught it, and it became a staff in his hand" (Ex. 4:3–4). Later on,

> The LORD said to Moses and Aaron, "When Pharaoh says to you, 'Prove yourselves by working a miracle,' then you shall say to Aaron, 'Take your staff and cast it down before Pharaoh, that it may become *a serpent*.'" So Moses and Aaron went to Pharaoh and did just as the LORD commanded. Aaron cast down his staff before Pharaoh and his servants, and it became *a serpent*. Then Pharaoh summoned the wise men and the sorcerers, and they, the magicians of Egypt, also did the same by their secret arts. For each man cast down his staff, and they became *serpents*. But *Aaron's staff swallowed up their staffs*. Still Pharaoh's heart was hardened, and he would not listen to them, as the LORD had said. (Ex. 7:8–13)

The Hebrew words for *serpent* in these two passages are different—*nahash* (snake) in Exodus 4:3 and *tannin* (serpent or dragon) in 7:9, 10, and 12. But the terms can be synonymous depending on the context, and in these contexts they refer to the same type of snake—especially since Exodus 7:15 uses the term *nahash*.[2] At the same time, this passage polemically presents the Lord as more powerful than the most chaotic form of evil—the *tannin*. The episode in 7:8–13 taunts Pharaoh, king of Egypt, as a weak dragon.

Aaron's staff likely turned into the cobra that the Egyptians featured on Pharaoh's kingly headgear: "Egyptian pharaohs wore headgear with an erect cobra in front, signifying divine power and protection."[3] That headgear displayed the *uraeus*—"a representation

---

2. Cf. John D. Currid, *Ancient Egypt and the Old Testament* (Grand Rapids, MI: Baker, 1997), 86–87; Eugene Carpenter, *Exodus 1–18*, Evangelical Exegetical Commentary (Bellingham, WA: Lexham, 2016), 364–65.

3. Robert C. Stallman, "נָחָשׁ," in *The New International Dictionary of Old Testament Theology and Exegesis*, ed. Willem VanGemeren, 5 vols. (Grand Rapids, MI: Zondervan, 1997), 3:85.

of a sacred serpent as an emblem of supreme power, worn on the headdresses of ancient Egyptian deities and sovereigns."[4]

John Currid, an Old Testament professor who is an expert in biblical archaeology and the ancient Near East, explains why the serpent symbolism in Exodus 7 is so significant:

> Probably the most important serpent worship was the cult of Uraeus centered in the city of Per-Wadjit in the delta. There a temple was built in the early dynastic period in honor of the Uraeus-goddess Wadjet. She personified the cobra and was the tutelary [i.e., protector] goddess of Lower Egypt. Wadjet served the same function as did the vulture-goddess Nekhbet, the tutelary deity of Upper Egypt. Those two goddesses represented all strength, power, and sovereignty in the two lands of ancient Egypt.
>
> Egyptian textual evidence declares that Pharaoh was able to control all Egypt because he was imbued with the power of the two goddesses. . . .
>
> The two goddesses and the sovereignty they imparted to Pharaoh were physically represented on the front of the king's crown in the form of an enraged female cobra. To the Egyptian the royal diadem was an object "charged with power and was, in fact, not always distinguished from the goddesses themselves." An inanimate object thought to be energized with divine sovereignty and potency, this uraeus came to be considered the emblem of Pharaoh's power. . . .
>
> So the serpent-crested diadem of Pharaoh symbolized all the power, sovereignty, and magic with which the gods endued the king. It was the emblem of his divine force. . . .

---

4. Catherine Soanes and Angus Stevenson, eds., *Concise Oxford English Dictionary*, 11th ed. (Oxford: Oxford University Press, 2004).

The Egyptians described Pharaoh as eternal, worthy of worship, and omniscient; he imbued Egypt with existence and power. They taught that he was *ka*, the life force and soul of Egypt. And the serpent-crested coronet symbolized his deification and majesty. When Moses had Aaron fling the rod-snake before Pharaoh, he was directly assaulting that token of Pharaonic sovereignty—the scene was one of polemical taunting. When Aaron's rod swallowed the staffs of the Egyptian magicians, Pharaonic deity and omnipotence were being denounced and rejected outright. Pharaoh's cobra-crested diadem had no power against Yahweh.[5]

Egyptians idolatrously venerated the serpent. They illustrate how Paul describes idolaters: "Claiming to be wise, they became fools, and exchanged the glory of *the immortal God for images resembling* mortal man and birds and animals and *creeping things*" (Rom. 1:22–23). The serpent was one of the gods of Egypt, and God stated what he intended to accomplish by battling Pharaoh: "*On all the gods of Egypt I will execute judgments*" (Ex. 12:12). So when Aaron's staff transformed into a serpent that swallowed up the serpents of Pharaoh's magicians, God was sending Pharaoh a strong message: *Egypt thinks Pharaoh is a mighty, immortal serpent, but God can easily swallow him up.* And that is exactly what God did to the Egyptian army in the Red Sea:

> Who is like you, O LORD, among the gods?
>> Who is like you, majestic in holiness,
>> awesome in glorious deeds, doing wonders?
> You stretched out your right hand;
>> *the earth swallowed them.* (Ex. 15:11–12; cf. 14:16, 26)

---

5. Currid, *Ancient Egypt*, 89, 91, 93–94.

"Swallowed" translates the same Hebrew word as in Exodus 7:12: "Aaron's staff *swallowed* up their staffs."

God spectacularly delivered his people from Egypt and its hard-hearted Pharaoh (Ex. 12–15). Later passages in Psalms and Isaiah refer to that exodus as God's defeating the serpent:

> Yet God my King is from of old,
>> working salvation in the midst of the earth.
> You *divided the sea* by your might [cf. Ex. 14:13, 16, 29–30;
>>> 15:2, 8, 13, 19];
>> you *broke the heads of the sea monsters on the waters.*
> You *crushed the heads of Leviathan*;
>> you *gave him as food for the creatures of the wilderness.*
>> (Ps. 74:12–14)

That poetry is a polemic against the gods. Canaanites boasted that Baal was more powerful than the dragon.[6] "The point here," explains Old Testament scholar Derek Kidner, "is that what Baal had claimed in the realm of myth, God had done in the realm of history—and done for his people, *working salvation.*"[7]

The Hebrew word *rahab* refers to a mythical sea monster (Job 9:13; 26:12; Ps. 89:10), and Isaiah equates it with the dragon to symbolize Egypt. Specifically, God redeemed his people from Egypt when they passed through the Red Sea.

> Awake, awake, put on strength,
>> O arm of the LORD;

---

6. Cf. John Day, *God's Conflict with the Dragon and the Sea: Echoes of a Canaanite Myth in the Old Testament*, University of Cambridge Oriental Publications 35 (Cambridge: Cambridge University Press, 1985), 1–18.

7. Derek Kidner, *Psalms 73–150: An Introduction and Commentary*, Tyndale Old Testament Commentaries 16 (Downers Grove, IL: InterVarsity Press, 1975), 297. Cf. Willem A. VanGemeren, *Psalms*, 2nd ed., Expositor's Bible Commentary 3 (Grand Rapids, MI: Zondervan, 2008), 573; Allen P. Ross, *A Commentary on the Psalms: Volume 2 (42–89)*, Kregel Exegetical Library (Grand Rapids, MI: Kregel, 2013), 586–87.

awake, as in days of old,
>   the generations of long ago.
> *Was it not you who cut Rahab in pieces,*
>   *who pierced the dragon?*
> Was it not you who dried up the sea,
>   the waters of the great deep,
> who made the depths of the sea a way
>   for the redeemed to pass over?
> And the ransomed of the LORD shall return
>   and come to Zion with singing;
> everlasting joy shall be upon their heads;
>   they shall obtain gladness and joy,
>   and sorrow and sighing shall flee away. (Isa. 51:9–11)

Isaiah mentions two exoduses here: (1) God redeemed his people from Egypt, and (2) God will redeem his people again by decisively defeating the dragon (compare Isa. 7:14 and Matt. 1:21–23; Hos. 11 and Matt. 2:13–15; see also Luke 9:30–31; Rev. 12:11).

GOD SENDS POISONOUS SNAKES AMONG HIS COMPLAINING PEOPLE IN THE WILDERNESS AND PROVIDES A CURSE-BEARING BRONZE SNAKE

When the Israelites complained that God delivered them from Egypt only to die in the wilderness, God sent poisonous snakes among them to provoke them to repent. It's as if God said to the complaining Israelites: "So you miss Egypt? Here you go. Have some snakes—the signature animal that Egypt idolatrously venerates."

> From Mount Hor they [i.e., the Israelites] set out by the way to the Red Sea, to go around the land of Edom. And the people became impatient on the way. And the people spoke

against God and against Moses, "Why have you brought us up out of *Egypt* to die in the wilderness? For there is no food and no water, and we loathe this worthless food." Then *the LORD sent fiery serpents among the people, and they bit the people, so that many people of Israel died.* And the people came to Moses and said, "We have sinned, for we have spoken against the LORD and against you. *Pray to the LORD, that he take away the serpents from us.*" So Moses prayed for the people. And the LORD said to Moses, "*Make a fiery serpent and set it on a pole, and everyone who is bitten, when he sees it, shall live.*" So *Moses made a bronze serpent and set it on a pole. And if a serpent bit anyone, he would look at the bronze serpent and live.* (Num. 21:4–9)

At least four items are significantly symbolic.

1. Looking at the bronze (or copper) snake symbolized faith in God. When snakebitten people looked at the bronze snake with faith, they were trusting that only God could deliver them from the consequences of their sin.

2. The bronze snake symbolized bearing the curse in the place of snakebitten and faith-filled Israelites. The serpent symbolized bearing a curse, not giving life.[8]

3. Lifting the snake on a pole symbolized that God would draw the curse away from his snakebitten and faith-filled people.

4. The snake on a military standard (ESV: "pole") symbolized that God had conquered Egypt and was protecting the Israelites.[9] Egyptians prized poisonous snakes as symbolizing Egypt's power (e.g., Pharaoh featured the Uraeus on his crown). The text doesn't

---

8. Contra James H. Charlesworth, *The Good and Evil Serpent: How a Universal Symbol Became Christianized*, The Anchor Yale Bible Reference Library (New Haven, CT: Yale University Press, 2010).

9. See Currid, *Ancient Egypt*, 150–54.

explicitly describe how Moses depicted the bronze snake on the pole, but it is possible that Moses depicted it as *impaled* on a military standard.

Later, Scripture draws three lessons from this incident.

1. *God's people must beware of idolatry.* The Israelites kept the bronze serpent in the temple, and about seven hundred years later they were tragically worshiping the bronze serpent instead of the one true God! Since they treated the bronze serpent as a fetish, King Hezekiah destroyed it: "He broke in pieces the bronze serpent that Moses had made, for until those days the people of Israel had made offerings to it (it was called *Nehushtan*)" (2 Kings 18:4). The ESV note explains, "*Nehushtan* sounds like the Hebrew for both *bronze* and *serpent*." Making offerings to a physical object is not the only way to commit idolatry. Many theologians such as Augustine, Martin Luther, John Calvin, Jonathan Edwards, and Tim Keller have pointed out that the human heart is an idol factory and that idolatry is behind all sin.[10]

2. *The curse-bearing bronze serpent is a type of Jesus on the cross.* Jesus explains, "As Moses lifted up the serpent in the wilderness, so must the Son of Man be lifted up, that whoever believes in him may have eternal life" (John 3:14–15). Typology works to understand how New Testament persons, events, and institutions (i.e., antitypes) fulfill Old Testament persons, events, and institutions (i.e., types) by repeating the Old Testament situations at a deeper, climactic level in salvation history (cf. Heb. 8:5; 10:1). God gave his faith-filled

---

10. See Timothy Keller, *Counterfeit Gods: The Empty Promises of Money, Sex, and Power, and the Only Hope That Matters* (New York: Dutton, 2009), xiv–xix, 171, 178–79, 202–3. Cf. Brian S. Rosner, "The Concept of Idolatry," *Themelios* 24, no. 3 (1999): 21–30; Rosner, "Idolatry," in *New Dictionary of Biblical Theology*, ed. T. Desmond Alexander and Brian S. Rosner (Downers Grove, IL: InterVarsity Press, 2000), 569–75; Rosner, *Greed as Idolatry: The Origin and Meaning of a Pauline Metaphor* (Grand Rapids, MI: Eerdmans, 2007); G. K. Beale, *We Become What We Worship: A Biblical Theology of Idolatry* (Downers Grove, IL: InterVarsity Press, 2008); Julian Hardyman, *Idols: God's Battle for Our Hearts* (Leicester: Inter-Varsity Press, 2010); Brad Bigney, *Gospel Treason: Betraying the Gospel with Hidden Idols* (Phillipsburg, NJ: P&R, 2012); David Powlison, "Revisiting Idols of the Heart and Vanity Fair," *Journal of Biblical Counseling* 27, no. 3 (2013): 37–68.

people physical and temporal life through the curse-bearing bronze snake, and God gives his faith-filled people spiritual and eternal life through the curse-bearing Son of Man on the cross. Moses lifted up the bronze snake on a military standard, and the Son of Man was lifted up on a cross (cf. John 8:28; 12:32–34). Like the bronze snake, Jesus bore the curse in the place of people who deserved it (cf. 2 Cor. 5:21; Gal. 3:13; 1 Pet. 2:24). Unlike the bronze snake, Jesus has life in himself (John 1:4; 5:26).[11]

3. *God's people must persevere by remembering him and not testing him.* The people of God must not forget their God, who delivered his people from Egypt and led them "through the great and terrifying wilderness, with its fiery serpents" (Deut. 8:11–19). "We must not put Christ to the test, as some of them did and were destroyed by *serpents*" (1 Cor. 10:9). Most of Israel was disqualified even though they experienced remarkable blessings from Yahweh. Christians today—who have also experienced remarkable blessings from Christ—must (like Paul) run the race so that they will not be disqualified (1 Cor. 9:24–10:11).

Egypt Is a Toothless Dragon

It was foolish for Israel to trust in Egypt instead of the Lord. God describes Egypt's "help" as "worthless and empty," so he labels her "Rahab who sits still" (Isa. 30:7). Egypt was a toothless dragon, a useless ally.

"Ah, stubborn children," declares the Lord,

"who carry out a plan, but not mine,

and who make an alliance, but not of my Spirit,

that they may add sin to sin;

---

11. D. A. Carson, *The Gospel according to John*, Pillar New Testament Commentary (Grand Rapids, MI: Eerdmans, 1991), 201–3; Edmund P. Clowney, *The Unfolding Mystery: Discovering Christ in the Old Testament*, 2nd ed. (Phillipsburg, NJ: P&R, 2013), 122–24.

who set out to go down to Egypt,
    without asking for my direction,
to take refuge in the protection of Pharaoh
    and to seek shelter in the shadow of Egypt!
Therefore shall the protection of Pharaoh turn to your
        shame,
    and the shelter in the shadow of Egypt to your
        humiliation. . . .

Through a land of trouble and anguish,
    from where come the lioness and the lion,
    the adder and the flying fiery serpent,
they carry their riches on the backs of donkeys,
    and their treasures on the humps of camels,
    to a people that cannot profit them.
Egypt's help is worthless and empty;
    therefore I have called her
    "Rahab who sits still." (Isa. 30:1–3, 6–7)

THE LORD WILL JUDGE EGYPT

Jeremiah prophesied that the Lord would use Babylon to judge Egypt:

She [i.e., Egypt] *makes a sound like a serpent gliding away;*
    for her enemies [i.e., Babylon] march in force
and come against her with axes
    like those who fell trees. (Jer. 46:22)

In 587 BC (shortly before Babylon conquered Jerusalem), the Lord commanded Ezekiel to prophesy against Egypt that the Lord would go on a fishing trip to the Nile River, which Pharaoh thought he owned:

> Behold, *I am against you,*
>> *Pharaoh king of Egypt,*
> *the great dragon* [NIV: "you great monster"] that lies
>> in the midst of his streams,
> that says, "My Nile is my own;
>> I made it for myself."
> *I will put hooks in your jaws,*
>> *and make the fish of your streams stick to your scales;*
> *and I will draw you up out of the midst of your streams,*
>> *with all the fish of your streams*
>> *that stick to your scales.*
> And I will cast you out into the wilderness,
>> you and all the fish of your streams;
> you shall fall on the open field,
>> and not be brought together or gathered.
> To the beasts of the earth and to the birds of the heavens
>> I give you as food.

Then all the inhabitants of Egypt shall know that I am the LORD.

Because you have been a staff of reed to the house of Israel, when they grasped you with the hand, you broke and tore all their shoulders; and when they leaned on you, you broke and made all their loins to shake. Therefore thus says the Lord GOD: Behold, *I will bring a sword upon you, and will cut off from you man and beast, and the land of Egypt shall be a desolation and a waste.* Then they will know that I am the LORD. (Ezek. 29:3–9)

God used Babylon to judge Egypt.

A few years after Jerusalem fell to Babylon in 587 BC, Egypt would be tempted to gloat that it had survived while Judah fell. In

585, the Lord commanded Ezekiel to lament over "Pharaoh king of Egypt" (Ezek. 32:2) by pronouncing that God will violently destroy the Egyptian dragon:

> You consider yourself a lion of the nations,
>> but *you are like a dragon* [Heb. *tannin*] in the seas;
> you burst forth in your rivers,
>> trouble the waters with your feet,
>> and foul their rivers.
> Thus says the Lord GOD:
>> *I will throw my net over you*
>> with a host of many peoples,
>> and *they will haul you up in my dragnet.*
> And I will cast you on the ground;
>> on the open field I will fling you,
> and will cause all the birds of the heavens to settle
>>> on you,
>> and *I will gorge the beasts of the whole earth with you.*
> I will strew your flesh upon the mountains
>> and fill the valleys with your carcass.
> *I will drench the land even to the mountains*
>> *with your flowing blood,*
>> and the ravines will be full of you.
> When I blot you out, I will cover the heavens
>> and make their stars dark;
> I will cover the sun with a cloud,
>> and the moon shall not give its light.
> All the bright lights of heaven
>> will I make dark over you,
>> and put darkness on your land,
>>> declares the Lord GOD.

I will trouble the hearts of many peoples, when *I bring your destruction* among the nations, into the countries that you have not known. (Ezek. 32:2–9)

Wicked Leaders in Canaan and Moab: Serpent Heads to Crush

God himself crushes the head of wicked leaders. Balaam prophesied,

I see him, but not now;
    I behold him, but not near:
a star shall come out of Jacob,
    and a scepter shall rise out of Israel;
it shall crush the forehead of Moab
    and break down all the sons of Sheth. (Num. 24:17)

King David defeated Moab (2 Sam. 8:2, 14), and the king who ultimately fulfills that prophecy is Jesus the Messiah, "the Root of David" who "has conquered" (Rev. 5:5).

Habakkuk 3 also refers to head-crushing and may portray God's enemies as dragons:

You went out for the salvation of your people,
    for the salvation of your anointed.
You crushed the head of the house of the wicked,
    laying him bare from thigh to neck.   *Selah* (Hab. 3:13)

"From thigh to neck" could read "from *tail* to neck," and it "appears to be a reference to the enemy in the form of a dragon."[12] If so, then Habakkuk 3:13 teaches that God saves his people from dragons.

God crushes his enemies.

---

12. Ralph L. Smith, *Micah–Malachi*, Word Biblical Commentary 32 (Dallas: Word, 1984), 116.

I will crush his [i.e., David's] *foes* before him
> and strike down those who hate him. (Ps. 89:23)

The Lord is at your right hand;
> *he will shatter* [NIV: "crush"] *kings* on the day of his
>> wrath.

He will execute judgment among the nations,
> filling them with corpses;

he will shatter chiefs [or *he will crush the head*]
> over the wide earth. (Ps. 110:5–6)

God is the one who ultimately crushes serpent heads, and he ordains that his people participate in the head-crushing.

But *God will strike the heads of his enemies,*
> the hairy crown of him who walks in his guilty ways.

The Lord said,
> "I will bring them back from Bashan,

I will bring them back from the depths of the sea,

that *you may strike your feet in their blood,*
> that the tongues of your dogs may have their portion
>> from the foe." (Ps. 68:21–23)

What follows highlights four episodes of God's crushing the heads of wicked leaders in Canaan and Moab. These stories connect to Genesis 3:14–15 regarding the cursed serpent, the serpent's offspring, and head-crushing. In each of the four episodes, God enables someone to courageously crush the head of one of the serpent's offspring.

JAEL DRIVES A PEG INTO SISERA'S TEMPLE

God cursed the Canaanites (Gen. 9:25). The Canaanites were Yahweh-hating idolaters, and they were serpent heads for God's people to crush when they entered the promised land. Sisera was a military commander for the Canaanite king Jabin.

> But Sisera fled away on foot to the tent of Jael, the wife of Heber the Kenite [i.e., Israelite relatives—cf. Judg. 1:16], for there was peace between Jabin the king of Hazor and the house of Heber the Kenite. And Jael came out to meet Sisera and said to him, "Turn aside, my lord; turn aside to me; do not be afraid." So he turned aside to her into the tent, and she covered him with a rug. And he said to her, "Please give me a little water to drink, for I am thirsty." So she opened a skin of milk and gave him a drink and covered him. And he said to her, "Stand at the opening of the tent, and if any man comes and asks you, 'Is anyone here?' say, 'No.'" But Jael the wife of Heber took a tent peg, and took a hammer in her hand. Then she went softly to him and *drove the peg into his temple until it went down into the ground while he was lying fast asleep from weariness. So he died.* And behold, as Barak was pursuing Sisera, Jael went out to meet him and said to him, "Come, and I will show you the man whom you are seeking." So he went in to her tent, and there lay Sisera dead, with the tent peg in his temple.
>
> So on that day *God subdued Jabin the king of Canaan* before the people of Israel. And the hand of the people of Israel pressed harder and harder against Jabin the king of Canaan, until *they destroyed Jabin king of Canaan.* (Judg. 4:17–24)

In Judges 5, Deborah and Barak praise the Lord with a song. They celebrate how God delivered the Israelites from the Canaanites, especially how Jael crushed Sisera:

> Most blessed of women be Jael,
> > the wife of Heber the Kenite,

of tent-dwelling women most blessed.
He asked for water and she gave him milk;
    she brought him curds in a noble's bowl.
She sent her hand to the tent peg
    and her right hand to the workmen's mallet;
she struck Sisera;
    she crushed his head;
    she shattered and pierced his temple.
Between her feet
    he sank, he fell, he lay still;
between her feet
    he sank, he fell;
where *he sank*,
    there he fell—dead. (Judg. 5:24–27)

The seed of the woman crushes the seed of the serpent. God saves his people by judging their enemies.[13]

A Woman Crushes Abimelech's Skull

Abimelech was not a Canaanite. He was a son of Jerubbaal (i.e., Gideon). But he wickedly murdered his brothers—potential rivals to the throne—to make himself a king in Canaan (Judg. 9:1–6). He experienced poetic justice when he attempted to burn down a strong tower within Shechem that was filled with men and women.

And Abimelech came to the tower and fought against it and drew near to the door of the tower to burn it with fire. And *a certain woman threw an upper millstone on Abimelech's head and crushed his skull*. Then he called quickly to the young man his armor-bearer and said to him, "Draw your sword

13. Cf. James M. Hamilton Jr., "The Skull Crushing Seed of the Woman: Inner-Biblical Interpretation of Genesis 3:15," *The Southern Baptist Journal of Theology* 10, no. 2 (2006): 35.

and kill me, lest they say of me, 'A woman killed him.'" And his young man thrust him through, and he died. And when the men of Israel saw that Abimelech was dead, everyone departed to his home. Thus *God returned the evil of Abimelech*, which he committed against his father in killing his seventy brothers. And *God also made all the evil of the men of Shechem return on their heads*, and upon them came the curse of Jotham the son of Jerubbaal. (Judg. 9:52–57)

The manly man Abimelech murdered his seventy brothers "on one stone" (Judg. 9:5), and he died in humiliation after one (nameless) woman hurled one stone on his head. Once again the seed of the woman crushes the seed of the serpent. Hamilton explains:

Like Cain, who was physically a seed of the woman but showed himself to be the seed of the serpent by killing his brother, Abimelech shows the lineage of his ethical character by killing seventy of his brothers (Judg 9:1–5; cf. also 9:34–49, where he slaughters his subjects [9:6]). Judgment falls on the seed of the serpent (Abimelech), however, when a woman throws a millstone on Abimelech's head (*rosh*) and his skull (*gulgolet*) is crushed (*ratsats*) (9:53).[14]

SAUL CRUSHES NAHASH THE SNAKE

The name *Nahash* means snake. The Spirit of God enabled Saul to lead the Israelites to crush this snake—Nahash the Ammonite.

Then *Nahash the Ammonite* went up and besieged Jabesh-gilead, and all the men of Jabesh said to *Nahash*, "Make a treaty with us, and we will serve you." But *Nahash the Ammonite* said to them, "On this condition I will make a treaty

---

14. Hamilton, "Skull Crushing Seed," 35.

with you, that I gouge out all your right eyes, and thus bring disgrace on all Israel." . . .

Now, behold, Saul was coming from the field behind the oxen. And Saul said, "What is wrong with the people, that they are weeping?" So they told him the news of the men of Jabesh. And *the Spirit of God rushed upon Saul* when he heard these words, and his anger was greatly kindled. He took a yoke of oxen and cut them in pieces and sent them throughout all the territory of Israel by the hand of the messengers, saying, "Whoever does not come out after Saul and Samuel, so shall it be done to his oxen!" Then the dread of the LORD fell upon the people, and they came out as one man. When he mustered them at Bezek, the people of Israel were three hundred thousand, and the men of Judah thirty thousand. And they said to the messengers who had come, "Thus shall you say to the men of Jabesh-gilead: 'Tomorrow, by the time the sun is hot, you shall have salvation.'" When the messengers came and told the men of Jabesh, they were glad. Therefore the men of Jabesh said, "Tomorrow we will give ourselves up to you, and you may do to us whatever seems good to you." And the next day Saul put the people in three companies. And they came into the midst of the camp in the morning watch and *struck down the Ammonites* until the heat of the day. And those who survived were scattered, so that no two of them were left together. (1 Sam. 11:1–2, 5–11)

The seed of the woman again crushes the seed of the serpent.

DAVID CRUSHES GOLIATH, THE GIANT DRAGON

In the famous story of David and Goliath, Goliath is a giant serpent who wears scaly armor and terrorizes God's people. God enables

David to conquer the dragon by crushing his head with a stone, with the result that Goliath falls facedown like Dagon (cf. 1 Sam. 5:3–4) and eats dust like the serpent (cf. Gen. 3:14). Then David cuts off Goliath's head with the giant's own sword. Note especially the italicized words in this famous story:

> Now the Philistines gathered their armies for battle. And they were gathered at Socoh, which belongs to Judah, and encamped between Socoh and Azekah, in Ephes-dammim. And Saul and the men of Israel were gathered, and encamped in the Valley of Elah, and drew up in line of battle against the Philistines. And the Philistines stood on the mountain on the one side, and Israel stood on the mountain on the other side, with a valley between them. And there came out from the camp of the Philistines *a champion named Goliath* of Gath, whose height was six cubits and a span. He had a helmet of bronze on his head, and *he was armed with a coat of mail*, and the weight of the coat was five thousand shekels of bronze. And he had bronze armor on his legs, and a javelin of bronze slung between his shoulders. The shaft of his spear was like a weaver's beam, and his spear's head weighed six hundred shekels of iron. And his shield-bearer went before him. He stood and shouted to the ranks of Israel, "Why have you come out to draw up for battle? Am I not a Philistine, and are you not servants of Saul? Choose a man for yourselves, and let him come down to me. If he is able to fight with me and kill me, then we will be your servants. But if I prevail against him and kill him, then you shall be our servants and serve us." And the Philistine said, "I defy the ranks of Israel this day. Give me a man, that we may fight together." When Saul and all Israel heard these words of the Philistine, they were dismayed and greatly afraid. . . .

And the Philistine moved forward and came near to David, with his shield-bearer in front of him. And when the Philistine looked and saw David, he disdained him, for he was but a youth, ruddy and handsome in appearance. And the Philistine said to David, "Am I a dog, that you come to me with sticks?" And *the Philistine cursed David by his gods.* The Philistine said to David, "Come to me, and I will give your flesh to the birds of the air and to the beasts of the field." Then David said to the Philistine, "You come to me with a sword and with a spear and with a javelin, but *I come to you in the name of the LORD of hosts, the God of the armies of Israel, whom you have defied. This day the LORD will deliver you into my hand, and I will strike you down and cut off your head. And I will give the dead bodies of the host of the Philistines this day to the birds of the air and to the wild beasts of the earth, that all the earth may know that there is a God in Israel,* and that all this assembly may know that the LORD saves not with sword and spear. For *the battle is the LORD's,* and he will give you into our hand."

When the Philistine arose and came and drew near to meet David, David ran quickly toward the battle line to meet the Philistine. And David put his hand in his bag and took out a stone and slung it and struck the Philistine on his forehead. *The stone sank into his forehead, and he fell on his face to the ground.*

So David prevailed over the Philistine with a sling and with a stone, and struck the Philistine and killed him. There was no sword in the hand of David. Then David ran and stood over the Philistine and took his sword and drew it out of its sheath and killed him and *cut off his head* with it. When the Philistines saw that their champion was dead, they fled.

> And the men of Israel and Judah rose with a shout and pursued the Philistines as far as Gath and the gates of Ekron, so that the wounded Philistines fell on the way from Shaaraim as far as Gath and Ekron. And the people of Israel came back from chasing the Philistines, and they plundered their camp. And *David took the head of the Philistine and brought it to Jerusalem*, but he put his armor in his tent. (1 Sam. 17:1–11, 41–54)

Goliath "was armed with a coat of mail" (17:5). Here are some more form-based ways to translate that phrase:

- Goliath "was clothed with armor *of scales*" (my form-based translation).
- Goliath "was clothed with *scale*-armor" (NASB).
- Goliath "wore a coat of *scale* armor" (NIV).

The Hebrew word translated "of scales" or "scale" (*qasqeset*) occurs seven other times in the Old Testament, and every time it refers to the scales of fish—including the dragon in the sea (Lev. 11:9, 10, 12; Deut. 14:9, 10; Ezek. 29:4 [2x]). God calls Pharaoh "the great dragon" with "scales (Ezek. 29:3–4). It is also significant that the word appears twice in Ezekiel 29:4 because 1 Samuel 17 and Ezekiel 29 parallel each other in at least three important ways.[15]

1. First Samuel 17:5 and Ezekiel 29:3–4 are the only two passages in the Bible that describe a *person* as having scales. God calls Pharaoh "the great dragon" with "scales" (Ezek. 29:3–4; see the above section "The Lord Will Judge Egypt," p. 79). Goliath is also covered in scales—just like a dragon.

2. First Samuel 17:46 and Ezekiel 29:5 use parallel phrases:

---

15. Cf. Brian Verrett, "The Serpent in Samuel: A Messianic Motif" (ThM thesis, Bethlehem College & Seminary, 2016), 46–49.

I will give the dead bodies of the host of the Philistines this day to the birds of the air and to the wild beasts of the earth. (1 Sam. 17:46)

To the beasts of the earth and to the birds of the heavens I give you as food. (Ezek. 29:5)

3. First Samuel 17:46 and Ezekiel 29:6 parallel each other:

. . . that all the earth may know that there is a God in Israel. (1 Sam. 17:46)

Then all the inhabitants of Egypt shall know that I am the LORD. (Ezek. 29:6)

The theological message of the David and Goliath story is that "the battle is the LORD's" (1 Sam. 17:47). God slays dragons. Once again the seed of the woman crushes the seed of the serpent.

It is surely no coincidence that when the seed of the woman named David lets fly his stone, the uncircumcised Philistine seed of the serpent who defied the armies of the living God gets struck [*nakhah*] on the forehead [*metsah*]. The stone sinks into his forehead [*wattitba haeven bemitsho*], and with a crushed head the Philistine falls dead (1 Sam 17:49). The collective seed of the woman are delivered from the seed of the serpent by the judgment administered through the singular seed of the woman.[16]

---

16. Hamilton, "Skull Crushing Seed," 35. *Forehead* (1 Sam. 17:49) translates the same Hebrew word that 17:6 renders "bronze *armor* on his legs" or "on his legs he wore bronze *greaves*" (NIV). So some Bible interpreters think David's stone hit Goliath's shin above the greave. I don't find the evidence for reading *greave* instead of *forehead* in 17:49 compelling. And in light of the head-crushing trajectory that begins in Gen. 3:14–15, it seems even more likely that *forehead* is the correct reading.

The King of Babylon: A Sea Monster

God would use Babylon to judge his rebellious people in Judah. This does not mean that Babylon would be innocent or exempt from punishment; it simply means that God ordained Babylon to accomplish his plan (cf. Jer. 27:1–15; the book of Habakkuk).[17] God describes Babylon as a sea monster and as poisonous serpents and adders, and he anticipates that his people in Judah will lament:

> "Nebuchadnezzar the king of Babylon has devoured me;
>> he has crushed me;
> he has made me an empty vessel;
>> *he has swallowed me like a monster*;
> he has filled his stomach with my delicacies;
>> he has rinsed me out.
> The violence done to me and to my kinsmen be upon
>>> Babylon,"
>> let the inhabitant of Zion say.
> "My blood be upon the inhabitants of Chaldea,"
>> let Jerusalem say. (Jer. 51:34–35)

God pronounces that he has ordained Babylon to serve as the instrument through which he judges his people:

> "The snorting of their [i.e., Babylon's] horses is heard
>> from Dan;
>> at the sound of the neighing of their stallions
>> the whole land quakes.
> They come and devour the land and all that fills it,
>> the city and those who dwell in it.
> For behold, *I am sending among you serpents*,

---

17. In due course, God will deal with Babylon for its brutality (Jer. 50:17–18, 34; 51:11, 24).

> adders that cannot be charmed,
> and they shall bite you,"
>> declares the LORD. (Jer. 8:16–17)

Babylon (like Egypt) is a serpent that opposes God and God's people.

King Herod: A Murderous Dragon

King Herod acts as a murderous dragon in the tragic story in Matthew 2:

> When they [i.e., the Magi] had departed, behold, an angel of the Lord appeared to Joseph in a dream and said, "Rise, take the child and his mother and *flee to Egypt*, and remain there until I tell you, for *Herod is about to search for the child, to destroy him*." And he rose and took the child and his mother by night and departed to Egypt, and remained there until the death of Herod. This was to fulfill what the Lord had spoken by the prophet, "Out of Egypt I called my son" [see Hos. 11:1].
>
> Then Herod, when he saw that he had been tricked by the wise men, became furious, and he *sent and killed all the male children in Bethlehem and in all that region who were two years old and under*, according to the time he had ascertained from the wise men. Then was fulfilled what was spoken by the prophet Jeremiah [see Jer. 31:15]:
>
>> "A voice was heard in Ramah,
>>> weeping and loud lamentation,
>> Rachel weeping for her children;
>>> she refused to be comforted, because they are no
>>> more." (Matt. 2:13–18)

Three instances of typology are notable here. As mentioned earlier, typology analyzes how New Testament persons, events, and institutions (i.e., antitypes) fulfill Old Testament persons, events, and institutions (i.e., types) by repeating the Old Testament situations at a deeper, climactic level in salvation history.[18]

1. *The* dragon energized Pharaoh, king of Egypt, as a murderous dragon to slaughter the Israelites' baby boys (Ex. 1:16–22), yet Moses escaped, became a refugee in Midian, and later delivered his people in the exodus from Egypt (Ex. 2–15). Here the same ultimate dragon energizes King Herod as a murderous dragon to slaughter the Israelites' baby boys in Bethlehem after the Messiah is born, yet the Messiah—the new and greater Moses—escapes, becomes a refugee in Egypt, and delivers his people in the ultimate second exodus (see Luke 9:31). His name is Jesus "for he will save his people from their sins" (Matt. 1:21).

Satan the murderous dragon energizes Herod to be a murderous dragon. Herod first employs the strategy of the snake—to deceive the wise men by telling them, "Go and search diligently for the child, and when you have found him, bring me word, that I too may come and worship him" (Matt. 2:8). But God warns the wise men in a dream not to return to Herod (Matt. 2:12). "Then Herod, when he saw that he had been tricked by the wise men, became furious" (Matt. 2:16). So Herod employs the strategy of the dragon—to devour. Herod is an offspring of the serpent.

2. God brought his disobedient son, Israel, out of Egypt (Hos. 11). Here God's obedient Son—Jesus, the new and greater Israel—retraces Israel's steps to succeed where they had failed.

---

18. On this passage (esp. Matt. 2:15), see Robert L. Plummer, "Righteousness and Peace Kiss: The Reconciliation of Authorial Intent and Biblical Typology," *The Southern Baptist Journal of Theology* 14, no. 2 (2010): 54–61; G. K. Beale, "The Use of Hosea 11:1 in Matthew 2:15: One More Time," *Journal of the Evangelical Theological Society* 55, no. 4 (2012): 697–715; Brent E. Parker, "The Israel-Christ-Church Relationship," in *Progressive Covenantalism: Charting a Course between Dispensational and Covenant Theologies*, ed. Stephen J. Wellum and Brent E. Parker (Nashville: B&H, 2016), 39–68.

3. The Israelite mothers lamented when the Babylonians exiled their children and slaughtered the ones who remained in Judah (Jer. 31:15; see also Isa. 49:15), but there was still hope for the Israelites because God promised that the exiles would return (Jer. 31:16–17). Here the Israelite mothers lament when Herod slaughters their baby boys, but there is still hope for God's people because the Messiah escapes and will inaugurate the new covenant (cf. Jer. 31:31–34)—despite the serpent's attempts to devour him.

Pharisees and Sadducees: A Brood of Vipers

Recall that a serpent has two major strategies: *deceive* and *devour*. Snakes deceive; dragons devour. Snakes tempt and lie; dragons attack and murder. Snakes backstab; dragons assault. At the beginning of Jesus's earthly ministry, Satan the snake attempts to deceive Jesus in the wilderness, and at the end of Jesus's earthly ministry, Satan the dragon murders Jesus by empowering Judas and the Jewish religious leaders.

In particular, the Pharisees and Sadducees are a brood of vipers—the serpent's offspring. Like their spiritual father—the serpent (cf. John 8:44)—the Pharisees and Sadducees first *tempt* Jesus (e.g., Matt. 16:1; 19:3; 22:18, 35; Mark 8:11; 10:2; 12:15; Luke 4:2; 11:16) and finally resort to *murdering* Jesus. Both John the Baptist and Jesus call them out for what they are—a hypocritical brood of vipers. What they teach is poisonous, and God will condemn them.

> But when he [i.e., John the Baptist] saw many of the Pharisees and Sadducees coming to his baptism, he said to them, "*You brood of vipers!* Who warned you to flee from the wrath to come? Bear fruit in keeping with repentance. And *do not presume to say to yourselves, 'We have Abraham as our father,'* for I tell you, God is able from these stones to raise up children for Abraham. Even now the axe is laid to the root of the trees.

Every tree therefore that does not bear good fruit is cut down and *thrown into the fire.*

"I baptize you with water for repentance, but he who is coming after me is mightier than I, whose sandals I am not worthy to carry. He will baptize you with the Holy Spirit and fire. His winnowing fork is in his hand, and he will clear his threshing floor and gather his wheat into the barn, but *the chaff he will burn with unquenchable fire.*" (Matt. 3:7–12; cf. Luke 3:7–9)

[Jesus said to the Pharisees,] "Either make the tree good and its fruit good, or make the tree bad and its fruit bad, for the tree is known by its fruit. *You brood of vipers!* How can you speak good, when *you are evil*? For out of the abundance of the heart the mouth speaks. The good person out of his good treasure brings forth good, and *the evil person out of his evil treasure brings forth evil.* I tell you, on the day of judgment people will give account for every careless word they speak, for by your words you will be justified, and *by your words you will be condemned.*" (Matt. 12:33–37)

[Jesus said,] "*Woe to you*, scribes and Pharisees, *hypocrites!* For you build the tombs of the prophets and decorate the monuments of the righteous, saying, 'If we had lived in the days of our fathers, we would not have taken part with them in shedding the blood of the prophets.' Thus you witness against yourselves that *you are sons of those who murdered the prophets.* Fill up, then, the measure of your fathers. *You serpents, you brood of vipers, how are you to escape being sentenced to hell?* Therefore I send you prophets and wise men and scribes, some of whom *you will kill and crucify,* and some *you will flog in your synagogues and persecute from town to town*, so that on you may come all the righteous blood shed on earth, from the blood of righteous Abel to the blood of Zechariah the son of Barachiah, whom *you murdered* between the sanctuary and the altar. Truly, I say to you, all these things will come upon this generation." (Matt. 23:29–36)

The Pharisees and Sadducees are the seed of the serpent—a poisonous, hypocritical, murderous brood of vipers. They are probably the most prominent false teachers in the New Testament (see the next section on false teachers).

False Teachers: Intruding Snakes

Paul explicitly connects the serpent with false teachers in two passages: 2 Corinthians 11 and Romans 16.

2 Corinthians 11:2–4, 13–15

For I feel a divine jealousy for you, since I betrothed you to one husband, to present you as a pure virgin to Christ. But I am afraid that *as the serpent deceived Eve by his cunning, your thoughts will be led astray* from a sincere and pure devotion to Christ. For if someone comes and proclaims another Jesus than the one we proclaimed, or if you receive a different spirit from the one you received, or if you accept a different gospel from the one you accepted, you put up with it readily enough. . . .

. . . For such men are *false apostles, deceitful workmen, disguising themselves as apostles of Christ.* And no wonder, for *even Satan disguises himself as an angel of light. So it is no surprise if his servants, also, disguise themselves as servants of righteousness.* Their end will correspond to their deeds.

Here's how Paul argues:

- *Concern (v. 2a).* I have a holy jealousy for you, Corinthians. I deeply love you; I am angry that false teachers are seducing you; and I fear what will happen to you if you continue on the wrong path.
- *Reason (v. 2b).* I betrothed you to one husband—namely, to the Messiah. But you are not being faithful to your husband.
- *Concern (v. 3).* I fear that as the snake cunningly deceived Eve's thinking to rebel against the Creator (cf. Gen. 3:6, 13; 1 Tim. 2:14), so false teachers will cunningly deceive your thinking to rebel against the Messiah. The snake damaged the first marriage (i.e., between Adam and Eve), and the snake is trying to damage the ultimate marriage to which the first marriage points (i.e., between Christ and his people).[19] "Satan always lies coiled ready to strike at the first sign of weakness (see [2 Cor.] 2:11) and to exchange sugarcoated lies for the unvarnished truth."[20]
- *Support (v. 4).* You are tolerating false teachers who proclaim a different Jesus than the crucified and risen Messiah, a different spirit than the Holy Spirit, a different gospel than the actual good news (cf. Gal. 1:8).
- *Explanation (v. 13).* These teachers are false apostles. They strategize to deceive you by disguising themselves as the Messiah's apostles.
- *Explanation (vv. 14–15a).* That's not surprising because these false teachers are Satan's servants. Satan deceitfully disguises himself as a shining angel from God, so his ser-

---

19. Earlier in this letter, Paul expresses concern that he and the Corinthians "would not be outwitted by Satan; for we are not ignorant of his designs" (2 Cor. 2:11).

20. David E. Garland, *2 Corinthians*, New American Commentary 29 (Nashville: Broadman & Holman, 1999), 462–63. Cf. D. A. Carson, *A Model of Christian Maturity: An Exposition of 2 Corinthians 10–13* (Grand Rapids, MI: Baker, 1984), 96–97.

vants deceitfully disguise themselves as God's servants who promote righteousness (cf. John 8:42–47). They are actually *enemies* of righteousness.[21]

- *Consequence (v. 15b).* On judgment day, the serpentine teachers will get what they deserve (cf. Matt. 7:15–23; 1 Cor. 3:17).

Romans 16:17–20

I appeal to you, brothers, to watch out for *those who cause divisions and create obstacles contrary to the doctrine that you have been taught*; avoid them. For such persons do not serve our Lord Christ, but their own appetites, and *by smooth talk and flattery they deceive the hearts of the naive*. For your obedience is known to all, so that I rejoice over you, but I want you to *be wise as to what is good and innocent as to what is evil. The God of peace will soon crush Satan under your feet.* The grace of our Lord Jesus Christ be with you.

Let's trace Paul's argument:

- *Warnings (vv. 17–19).*
  - *Warning (v. 17).* Beware and avoid false teachers. False teachers sinfully divide God's people and teach error that leads people to apostatize.
  - *Reasons (v. 18).* They idolatrously serve themselves (not our Lord, the Messiah), and like the snake they deceive the naive with enticing false teaching by smooth talk and clever rhetoric.

---

21. Compare how Paul addresses the false prophet Bar-Jesus: "Saul, who was also called Paul, filled with the Holy Spirit, looked intently at him and said, 'You *son of the devil*, you *enemy of all righteousness, full of all deceit and villainy*, will you not stop *making crooked the straight paths of the Lord*?'" (Acts 13:9–10). Satan is "the prince of the power of the air, the spirit that is now at work in *the sons of disobedience*" (Eph. 2:2). Satan is the master counterfeiter, and he uses false teachers to deceitfully accomplish his evil plan: "The god of this world has blinded the minds of the unbelievers, to keep them from seeing the light of the gospel of the glory of Christ" (2 Cor. 4:4).

- *Commendation/warning (v. 19a).* I rejoice that false teachers haven't deceived you. *Implied warning:* Since everyone knows about how you are obeying our Lord the Messiah, false teachers are likely planning to target you.

- *Warning (v. 19b).* You must be on guard to be wise about what's good and innocent about what's evil. Don't be innocent about what's good; you must wisely discern truth from error. Or as Jesus put it, "Be wise as serpents and innocent as doves" (Matt. 10:16).

- *Promise (v. 20a).* The God who brings *shalom* will soon crush Satan (and his false-teaching minions) under your feet (cf. Gen. 3:15; Ps. 8:6; 110:1). *Implied exhortation:* Therefore, heed my warnings in Romans 16:17–19—that is, persevere in avoiding false teachers until God finally crushes the serpent that energizes all false teachers. Satan and his false teachers won't deceive people forever. God will soon crush *the* adversary, who empowers other adversaries. And God's people will share in the victory. It'll be like Tolkien's *The Lord of the Rings*: When you finally defeat Sauron, you defeat Sauron's army. When you finally defeat Satan, you defeat Satan's minions.

- *Prayer (v. 20b).* May the Messiah's grace enable you to persevere in avoiding false teachers.

OTHER WARNINGS AGAINST FALSE TEACHERS

Satan the snake deploys false teachers to infiltrate God's people as intruding snakes. That's why the New Testament repeatedly warns God's people to beware of these deceitful snakes.

Beware of *false prophets*, who *come to you in sheep's clothing but inwardly are ravenous wolves*. (Matt. 7:15)

Yet because of *false brothers secretly brought in*—who *slipped in to spy out our freedom* that we have in Christ Jesus, so that they might bring us into slavery—to them we did not yield in submission even for a moment, so that the truth of the gospel might be preserved for you. . . .

For freedom Christ has set us free; stand firm therefore, and *do not submit again to a yoke of slavery*. (Gal. 2:4–5; 5:1)

See to it that no one takes you captive by *philosophy* and *empty deceit*, according to human tradition, according to *the elemental spirits of the world*, and not according to Christ. (Col. 2:8)

Now the Spirit expressly says that in later times some will depart from the faith by devoting themselves to *deceitful spirits* and *teachings of demons*, through *the insincerity of liars whose consciences are seared*, who forbid marriage and require abstinence from foods that God created to be received with thanksgiving by those who believe and know the truth. (1 Tim. 4:1–3)

But false prophets also arose among the people, just as there will be false teachers among you, who *will secretly bring in destructive heresies*, even denying the Master who bought them, bringing upon themselves swift destruction. And many will follow their sensuality, and because of them the way of truth will be blasphemed. And in their greed *they will exploit you with false words*. . . .

. . . They are blots and blemishes, *reveling in their deceptions*, while they feast with you. They have eyes full of adultery, insatiable for sin. They entice unsteady souls. They have hearts trained in greed. Accursed children!

. . . For, speaking loud boasts of folly, *they entice by sensual passions of the flesh* those who are barely escaping from those who live in error. *They promise them freedom*, but they themselves are slaves of corruption. For whatever overcomes a person, to that he is enslaved. (2 Pet. 2:1–3, 13–14, 18–20)

For many *deceivers* have gone out into the world, those who do not confess the coming of Jesus Christ in the flesh. Such a one is the *deceiver* and the *antichrist*. (2 John 7; cf. 1 John 2:18–27)

Beloved, although I was very eager to write to you about our common salvation, I found it necessary to write appealing to you to contend for the faith that was once for all delivered to the saints. For *certain people have crept in unnoticed* who long ago were designated for this condemnation, ungodly people, who pervert the grace of our God into sensuality and deny our only Master and Lord, Jesus Christ. (Jude 3–4)

Church leaders must not only *beware of* false teachers. They must also *rebuke* them, because shepherds protect the sheep.[22]

[An elder or overseer] must hold firm to the trustworthy word as taught, so that he may be able to give instruction in sound doctrine and also to *rebuke those who contradict it.*

For there are many who are insubordinate, empty talkers and *deceivers*, especially those of the circumcision party. They must be silenced, since they are upsetting whole families by teaching for shameful gain what they ought not to teach. One

---

22. Shepherds must know, feed, lead, and protect the sheep. On protecting the sheep, see Timothy Z. Witmer, *The Shepherd Leader: Achieving Effective Shepherding in Your Church* (Phillipsburg, NJ: P&R, 2010), 169–89.

of the Cretans, a prophet of their own, said, "Cretans are always liars, evil beasts, lazy gluttons." This testimony is true. Therefore rebuke them sharply, that they may be sound in the faith, not devoting themselves to Jewish myths and the commands of people who turn away from the truth. (Titus 1:9–14)

False teaching is a serious threat to God's people. That's why those who shepherd God's church must be able to both teach and defend what is true (Titus 1:9).

Satan is *the* snake, the ultimate deceiver. His human and demonic minions are his offspring—other snakes with the mission to intrude and deceive God's people. One of the snake's strategies to accomplish that evil plan is through false teachers and false teaching.

Conclusion

Satan is the ultimate serpent, and he energizes other serpents to craftily deceive and devour people. The Bible depicts at least six categories of such serpents: (1) Egypt and its Pharaoh, (2) wicked leaders in Canaan and Moab, (3) the king of Babylon, (4) King Herod, (5) Pharisees and Sadducees, and (6) other false teachers.

4

The Devouring Dragon in
Revelation 12 and 20

At the end of this age, Satan's strategy is not merely to deceive as the snake but also to devour as the dragon. A bookend along with Genesis 3 in its reference to the deceitful snake, the book of Revelation describes Satan in apocalyptic terms as the dragon (among other titles).[1] The end of the Bible's story teaches at least thirteen notable truths about the dragon.

The Dragon Is the Ancient Serpent

And the *great dragon* was thrown down, that *ancient serpent*, who is called the *devil* and *Satan*, the *deceiver* of the whole world. (Rev. 12:9)

---

1. On interpreting symbols in apocalyptic literature, see G. K. Beale, *The Book of Revelation: A Commentary on the Greek Text*, The New International Greek Testament Commentary (Grand Rapids, MI: Eerdmans, 1999), 50–69; Grant R. Osborne, *Revelation*, Baker Exegetical Commentary on the New Testament (Grand Rapids, MI: Baker Academic, 2002), 15–18; Alan S. Bandy, "The Hermeneutics of Symbolism: How to Interpret the Symbols of John's Apocalypse," *The Southern Baptist Journal of Theology* 14, no. 1 (2010): 46–59; Thomas R. Schreiner, "Revelation," in *Ephesians–Philemon*, ESV Expository Commentary 12 (Wheaton, IL: Crossway, 2018), 530–31.

The accuser of our brothers has been thrown down, *who accuses* them day and night before our God. (Rev. 12:10)

And when the *dragon* saw that he had been thrown down to the earth, he pursued the woman who had given birth to the male child. But the woman was given the two wings of the great eagle so that she might fly from the *serpent* into the wilderness, to the place where she is to be nourished for a time, and times, and half a time. The *serpent* poured water like a river out of his mouth after the woman, to sweep her away with a flood. But the earth came to the help of the woman, and the earth opened its mouth and swallowed the river that the *dragon* had poured from his mouth. Then the *dragon* became furious with the woman and went off to make war on the rest of her offspring. (Rev. 12:13–17)

And he seized the *dragon*, that *ancient serpent*, who is the *devil* and *Satan*, and bound him for a thousand years. (Rev. 20:2)

Six labels apply to the same evil person:

1. the dragon (Gk. *ho drakōn*)
2. the ancient serpent (Gk. *ho ophis ho archaios*; alludes to Gen. 3)
3. the devil (Gk. *Diabolos*—the slanderer)
4. Satan (Gk. *ho Satanas*—the adversary)
5. the deceiver (Gk. *ho planōn*)
6. the accuser of our brothers (Gk. *ho katēgōr tōn adelphōn*)

The dragon in Revelation is the same serpent the Old Testament depicts as God's enemy.[2] This dragon seeks to "devour" (12:4), but he also seeks to *deceive*. As the ancient serpent—the devil and Satan—he is "the deceiver of the whole world" (12:9), the one who deceives the nations (20:3, 7, 10).

---

2. Cf. Beale, *Revelation*, 634–35.

The Dragon Is a Murderer

And another sign appeared in heaven: behold, a great *red* dragon . . . (Rev. 12:3)

Red symbolizes blood to connote that the dragon is a murderer. Two other figures in Revelation are fiery red because they symbolize bloody murder.

1. The one riding a "bright red" horse "was permitted to take peace from the earth, so that people should slay one another, and he was given a great sword" (6:4; cf. 6:9–10).

2. The woman on a *scarlet* beast wears *scarlet* because she murders God's people:

> I saw a woman sitting on a *scarlet* beast that was full of blasphemous names, and it had seven heads and ten horns. The woman was arrayed in purple and *scarlet*, and adorned with gold and jewels and pearls, holding in her hand a golden cup full of abominations and the impurities of her sexual immorality. And on her forehead was written a name of mystery: "Babylon the great, mother of prostitutes and of earth's abominations." And I saw the woman, *drunk with the blood of the saints, the blood of the martyrs of Jesus.* (Rev. 17:3–6)

The dragon is fiery red because the dragon murders God's people. "He was a murderer from the beginning," asserts Jesus (John 8:44).

The Dragon Is Powerful

And another sign appeared in heaven: behold, a *great* red dragon, with seven heads and *ten horns*, and on his heads *seven diadems*. (Rev. 12:3)

The dragon is *great*. The ten horns symbolize great power and ruling authority (cf. Dan. 7:7–8, 19–27), and the seven diadems symbolize that his great power extends over the entire earth. The dragon is "the deceiver *of the whole world*" (Rev. 12:9). "The dragon is the power behind all idolatrous human rule."[3]

The Dragon Plans to Devour the Messiah

And a great sign appeared in heaven: a woman clothed with the sun, with the moon under her feet, and on her head a crown of twelve stars. She was pregnant and was crying out in birth pains and the agony of giving birth. And another sign appeared in heaven: behold, a great red dragon, with seven heads and ten horns, and on his heads seven diadems. His tail swept down a third of the stars of heaven and cast them to the earth. And *the dragon stood before the woman who was about to give birth, so that when she bore her child he might devour it*. She gave birth to a male child, one who is to rule all the nations with a rod of iron. (Rev. 12:1–4)

The male child is Jesus the Messiah, who rules with a rod of iron (Ps. 2:9; Rev. 2:27; 19:15). The dragon plans to thwart God's master plan in Genesis 3:15 by devouring the Messiah.

The dragon's "tail swept down a third of the stars of heaven and cast them to the earth" (Rev. 12:4). This alludes to the cosmic battle in Daniel 8:10, where a little horn "grew great, even to the host of heaven. And some of the host and some of the stars it threw down to the ground and trampled on them." D. A. Carson explains what's happening in Revelation 12:

This is not some form of mistaken ancient cosmology demonstrating that the biblical authors were woefully ignorant of scientific facts. Rather, this is part of apocalyptic metaphor

---

3. Richard Bauckham, "Revelation," in *The Oxford Bible Commentary*, ed. John Barton and John Muddiman (Oxford: Oxford University Press, 2001), 1296.

that derives from Hebrew poetry in which all of nature gets involved in everything. When things go well, the hills dance and the trees clap their hands. When things are bad, the stars fall from the sky, and nature falls into disarray. This is exactly what happens here. Satan is about to attempt something that is utterly catastrophic, so his tail swings around and a third of the universe collapses.[4]

While the woman is in labor, the dragon prepares to ravenously eat up the child. The image is revolting—and rightly so because that is how we should feel about the dragon.

Remember when King Herod so desperately wanted to murder the Messiah that he murdered all the boys in Bethlehem who were two years old or under (Matt. 2:16)? Only a monster could do such a thing. And that's exactly who was behind Herod's revolting plan—the dragon.

The Dragon Fails to Devour the Messiah

But her child was caught up to God and to his throne. (Rev. 12:5)

Just as the Narnian white witch tried to defeat Aslan by murdering him on the stone table, the dragon tries to defeat the Messiah by murdering him on the cross. But the next day Aslan rises from the stone table. And on the third day, the Messiah rises from the grave and later ascends to the Father's right hand. The serpent defeated Adam under a tree ("the tree of the knowledge of good and evil"—Gen. 2:17), and the new and greater Adam defeats the serpent on a tree—a cross for executing criminals. "With profound irony," early Christians spoke "of Jesus reigning from the cross."[5] The dragon fails to devour the Messiah.

---

4. D. A. Carson, *Scandalous: The Cross and Resurrection of Jesus* (Wheaton, IL: Crossway, 2010), 83–84.

5. Carson, *Scandalous*, 20. Justin Martyr was convinced that Ps. 96:10 should say not merely "The Lord reigns!" but instead "The Lord reigns *from the wood*" (*Dialogue with Trypho*, §73). Augustine quotes Justin and adds, "Who is it who fighteth with wood? Christ. With His cross

The Dragon and His Angels Get Thrown Down to Earth

Now war arose in heaven, Michael and his angels fighting against the dragon. And the dragon and his angels fought back, but *he was defeated*, and *there was no longer any place for them in heaven*. And *the great dragon was thrown down*, that ancient serpent, who is called the devil and Satan, the deceiver of the whole world—*he was thrown down to the earth, and his angels were thrown down with him*. And I heard a loud voice in heaven, saying, "Now the salvation and the power and the kingdom of our God and the authority of his Christ have come, for *the accuser of our brothers has been thrown down*, who accuses them day and night before our God." (Rev. 12:7–10)

Satan used to have access to God in the midst of other angels. In the prologue to the book of Job, Satan comes into God's presence and accuses Job of being a hypocrite—of serving God only because God in turn blesses Job so generously (Job 1–2). But now Satan can no longer accuse God's people in God's presence as he did in the past. He no longer has direct access to God, because God's angels threw Satan and his demons down to earth.

When did Satan get thrown down to earth? It happened when the Son of God became human, lived in a perfectly righteous way, sacrificially died for sinners, and rose again. That triumph decisively defeated Satan (see John 12:31; Col. 2:15). "Michael didn't triumph over the devil in his own strength. He cast him out of heaven because of the death of Christ, because of the victory won at the cross."[6]

He hath vanquished kings." Augustine, *Saint Augustin: Expositions on the Psalms*, vol. 8 in *Nicene and Post-Nicene Fathers of the Christian Church*, Series 1, ed. Philip Schaff (Grand Rapids, MI: Eerdmans, 1997), 471.

6. Thomas R. Schreiner, "What Does Revelation 12 Teach Us about the Cross of Christ and Persecution?," *The Southern Baptist Journal of Theology* 18, no. 1 (2014): 153.

The Dragon Is Conquered on the Basis of the Blood of the Lamb and the Word of the Saints' Testimony

And *they have conquered him by the blood of the Lamb and by the word of their testimony*, for they loved not their lives even unto death. Therefore, rejoice, O heavens and you who dwell in them!" (Rev. 12:11–12a)

The dragon is powerful, but someone who is all-powerful conquers him. On what basis? "By the blood of the Lamb and by the word of their testimony."

1. *The blood of the Lamb.* God's people conquer the dragon on the basis of the blood of the Lamb. The word for "lamb" (Gk. *arnion*) occurs twenty-nine times in Revelation out of thirty total times in the New Testament. The Lamb in Revelation is not an ordinary sacrificial lamb. The Lamb symbolizes both Jesus's bloody death *and* his triumphant victory. The Lamb is standing "as though it had been slain, with seven horns and with seven eyes" (5:6). This Lamb has conquered as "the Lion of the tribe of Judah, the Root of David" (5:5). God's enemies "will make war on the Lamb, and the Lamb will conquer them, for he is Lord of lords and King of kings" (17:14). And the Lamb's blood cleanses his people from their sins: "They have washed their robes and made them white in the blood of the Lamb" (7:14). The only basis on which God's people can approach him is the blood of the Lamb. Jesus the Messiah is "the firstborn of the dead" and the one "who loves us and has freed us from our sins by his blood" (1:5).

Jesus is the ultimate serpent crusher, and he decisively crushed the dragon by being "*crushed* for our iniquities" (Isa. 53:5). Jesus was crushed according to God's master plan: "it was the will of the LORD to *crush* him" (Isa. 53:10; cf. Acts 2:23–24; 4:27–28). God's people participate in crushing the dragon based on Jesus the Messiah's being crushed for their sins.

2. *The word of their testimony*. The gospel is a weapon in spiritual warfare. God's people conquer the dragon on the basis of the word of their testimony. The good news about the Lamb advances when God's people proclaim it—even if it costs them their lives (cf. Rev. 2:10; 6:9). They live in light of what Jesus commanded: "Do not fear those who kill the body but cannot kill the soul. Rather fear him who can destroy both soul and body in hell" (Matt. 10:28).

The Dragon Furiously Persecutes God's People

> And a great sign appeared in heaven: a woman clothed with the sun, with the moon under her feet, and on her head a crown of twelve stars. She was pregnant and was crying out in birth pains and the agony of giving birth. (Rev. 12:1–2)

> And the woman *fled* into the wilderness, where she has a place prepared by God, in which she is to be nourished for 1,260 days. (Rev. 12:6)

> But woe to you, O earth and sea, for the devil has come down to you in *great wrath, because he knows that his time is short*!
> And when the dragon saw that he had been thrown down to the earth, *he pursued the woman* who had given birth to the male child. But the woman was given the two wings of the great eagle so that she might *fly* from the serpent into the wilderness, to the place where she is to be nourished for a time, and times, and half a time. *The serpent poured water like a river out of his mouth after the woman, to sweep her away with a flood.* But the earth came to the help of the woman, and the earth opened its mouth and swallowed the river that the dragon had poured from his mouth. Then *the dragon became furious with the woman and went off to make war on the rest of her offspring*, on those who keep the

commandments of God and hold to the testimony of Jesus. And he stood on the sand of the sea. (Rev. 12:12–17)

Two symbols are noteworthy here: Who is the woman, and what are the 1,260 days? (See the next section below, "The Dragon Cannot Destroy God's People," p. 116, for a third question: What is the wilderness?)

1. *The woman symbolizes the people of God.* The woman initially may appear to be Mary the mother of Jesus, since she gives birth to the Messiah (Rev. 12:1–5). But as apocalyptic literature sometimes does, the passage later explains whom the woman symbolizes: "Then the dragon became furious with the woman and went off to make war on the rest of her offspring, on those who keep the commandments of God and hold to the testimony of Jesus" (12:17). The woman refers not only to Mary but also to the people of God, the entire messianic community, the collective seed of the woman (Gen. 3:15). One metaphor the Bible uses for the messianic community is *mother* (e.g., Isa. 54:1; Gal. 4:26). Carson explains:

> The Messiah springs from this mother, out of this woman, out of this messianic community. The messianic community gives birth to this child, and then the messianic community continues. The messianic community's children are the ones being persecuted in Revelation 12:17—and this side of the cross, the messianic community's children are Christians.
>
> The woman is "clothed with the sun" (v. 1); she is utterly radiant. Her feet on the moon suggest dominion. The "twelve stars on her head" are probably evocative of both the twelve tribes of the old covenant and the twelve apostles of the new, representing the fullness of the people of God. (Jesus links these two groups of twelve in Matthew 19.)

But the important thing for the drama is that she is pregnant: "She was pregnant and cried out in pain as she was about to give birth" (v. 2). Descriptions such as this generated the expression "the birth pains of the Messiah." This expression did not refer to the pains that the Messiah himself suffered, but the pains of the messianic community as the Messiah came to birth [e.g., Isa. 26:17].[7]

2. *The 1,260 days symbolize a period of intense suffering for God's people before God delivers them.* The book of Revelation refers to this three-and-a-half-year period in three ways:

- forty-two months (in which an ideal month is thirty days) (Rev. 11:2; 13:5)
- 1,260 days (Rev. 11:3; 12:6)
- a time (i.e., one year) and times (i.e., two years) and half a time (i.e., half a year) (Rev. 12:14; cf. Dan. 7:25; 12:7)

A three-and-a-half-year period symbolizes a time of intense suffering. That is how long the Maccabean Revolt took before the Jews became an independent nation again in 164 BC, and the Jews interpreted that time period as fulfilling what Daniel prophesied. The Jews suffered intensely under Antiochus IV Epiphanes, a Seleucid king who blasphemously sacrificed pigs in the Jerusalem temple. Again, Carson explains:

Thus, for Jews and Christians alike, three and a half years became emblematic of a period of intense suffering (of whatever duration) before God manifests himself in saving power. Of course, when John was writing this book, the Maccabean Revolt was more than two centuries behind him, but the point is

---

7. Carson, *Scandalous*, 81. Cf. Beale, *Revelation*, 628–32.

that the 1,260 days had become emblematic for any period of severe suffering. John uses the expression to refer to the *entire* period of suffering between Jesus' first and second advents. It is the period when there will be suffering, opposition, attack, and death. But ultimately there will be vindication at the end as God moves in.[8]

But for now, the dragon is raging. And he is raging against God's people. The story that began in Genesis 3:15 continues—enmity between the snake's offspring and the woman's offspring. Christ has *already* defeated the dragon, but he has *not yet* finally defeated him. That is why theologians describe the kingdom of God right now as *already but not yet*.

The kingdom of God is God's rule over his people and the entire created order. The Jewish apocalyptic movement during the Second Temple period (about 516 BC–AD 70) sharply divided the sin-dominated present age from the age to come when the Messiah conquers sin and eradicates its presence. The popular Jewish view of the kingdom was that God would become King and then vindicate the Jews by conquering their enemies. But Jesus spoke of the kingdom as already here in his person and teaching though not yet *fully* here because he has not yet fully consummated his rule. His coming inaugurated the age to come but did not yet eradicate sin's presence; that will happen in the future when Jesus returns.

That's where we live as Christians right now—between Jesus's first and second comings. Or to use Oscar Cullmann's analogy from World War II, Christians now live between D-Day (June 6, 1944) and V-E Day (May 8, 1945).[9] In World War II, on D-Day the allies decisively defeated their enemy. Victory for the allies was inevitable.

---

8. Carson, *Scandalous*, 89.

9. Oscar Cullmann, *Christ and Time: The Primitive Christian Conception of Time and History*, 2nd ed., trans. Floyd V. Filson (Philadelphia: Westminster, 1964), 141–42, 145–46.

But the war wasn't over yet. *Some of the most gruesome fighting in the war followed D-Day.* It was not until V-E Day (Victory in Europe Day) that the war officially ended. D-Day represents when Jesus decisively defeated Satan in his life, cross-work, resurrection, and ascension, and V-E Day represents when Jesus will return to earth to consummate his victory. Right now we are living in that period between D-Day and V-E Day. The war is not yet over. Jesus has already won the victory, but he has not yet consummated it. The kingdom is *already* but also *not yet*. And like Adolf Hitler after D-Day, *the dragon is raging because he knows he doesn't have long* (Rev. 12:12). He knows that Christ has decisively defeated him, so he is taking out his rage on Christ's church by attempting to deceive them (with lies and false teaching) and to devour them (with persecution).

The Dragon Cannot Destroy God's People

But *the woman was given the two wings of the great eagle* so that she might fly from the serpent into the wilderness, to the place where *she is to be nourished* for a time, and times, and half a time. The serpent poured water like a river out of his mouth after the woman, to sweep her away with a flood. But *the earth came to the help of the woman*, and the earth opened its mouth and swallowed the river that the dragon had poured from his mouth. (Rev. 12:14–16)

The wilderness symbolizes a place where God tests, protects, and miraculously nourishes his people. This exile-exodus theme progresses throughout the Bible's storyline (see comments on Gen. 3:22–24 in chap. 1, under "God Banishes Adam and Eve from the Garden of Eden," p. 44). The wilderness alludes to the forty challenging years Israel spent in the desert after God delivered them from slavery to Egypt. (It is no accident that the devil tempted Jesus *in the wilderness* after Jesus fasted *forty* days and nights [Matt. 4:1–2].) When Israel was in the wilderness before they entered the promised land, God miraculously provided for them—manna, quail, water, sandals that did not wear out. God simultaneously tested and nourished his people (cf. Deut. 8:2–5).

The wilderness that the woman flees to in Revelation 12 is "a place prepared by God" (12:6), a place where "she is to be nourished" (12:6, 14). It is where God simultaneously tests and nourishes his people. God miraculously protects them from the dragon's fury. The dragon cannot destroy God's people. That encourages them to persevere when the dragon tempts and persecutes them.

After God delivered Israel from slavery in Egypt, he told them, "You yourselves have seen what I did to the Egyptians, and how I bore you on eagles' wings and brought you to myself" (Ex. 19:4). And when God promised to deliver Israel from exile in Babylon (the second exodus), he told them,

> They who wait for the LORD shall renew their strength;
> > they shall mount up with wings like eagles. (Isa. 40:31)

And here once again God gives his people "the two wings of the great eagle so that she might fly from the serpent into the wilderness" (Rev. 12:14). The God-given wings symbolize that God protects and delivers his people.[10]

The Dragon Empowers the Beast

> And I saw a beast rising out of the sea, with ten horns and seven heads, with ten diadems on its horns and blasphemous names on its heads. And the beast that I saw was like a leopard; its feet were like a bear's, and its mouth was like a lion's mouth. And *to it the dragon gave his power and his*

---

10. Cf. Beale, *Revelation*, 643–50, 669–71.

throne and great authority. One of its heads seemed to have a mortal wound, but its mortal wound was healed, and the whole earth marveled as they followed the beast. And they worshiped the dragon, for *he had given his authority to the beast*, and they worshiped the beast, saying, "Who is like the beast, and who can fight against it?" (Rev. 13:1–4)

The dragon is God's chief adversary, and he forms a counterfeit trinity to rival the real Trinity (see Rev. 16:13; 20:10):

1. the dragon (i.e., Satan)
2. the first beast, which rises out of the sea (Rev. 13:1–4)
3. the second beast, which rises out of the earth—the false prophet (Rev. 13:11–18)

The dragon empowers the first beast to accomplish his evil purposes: "To it the dragon gave his power and his throne and great authority" (Rev. 13:2). This beast rises out of the sea, which symbolizes evil and chaos (cf. Dan. 7:2–3; Rev. 21:1). The dragon-empowered beast symbolizes Satan-empowered empires that persecute God's people.[11]

The Dragon Is Bound for a Thousand Years

Then I saw an angel coming down from heaven, holding in his hand the key to the bottomless pit and a great chain. And *he seized the dragon, that ancient serpent, who is the devil and Satan, and bound him for a thousand years, and threw him into the pit, and shut it and sealed it over him, so that he might not deceive the nations any longer, until the thousand years were ended*. After that he must be released for a little while.

Then I saw thrones, and seated on them were those to whom the authority to judge was committed. Also I saw the

---

11. Cf. Beale, *Revelation*, 680–95.

souls of those who had been beheaded for the testimony of Jesus and for the word of God, and those who had not worshiped the beast or its image and had not received its mark on their foreheads or their hands. They came to life and reigned with Christ for a thousand years. The rest of the dead did not come to life until the thousand years were ended. This is the first resurrection. Blessed and holy is the one who shares in the first resurrection! Over such the second death has no power, but they will be priests of God and of Christ, and they will reign with him for a thousand years. (Rev. 20:1–6)

Revelation 20:2–7 refers to a period of a "thousand years" six times. Theologians refer to this period of time as *the millennium*. Christians have disagreed on the nature of the millennium. There are three major views:[12]

1. *Premillennialism.* The millennium is the long period (perhaps a literal thousand years) when King Jesus will rule on earth. Jesus will return *before* the millennium (hence *pre*millennialism).[13]

2. *Postmillennialism.* The millennium is a golden age on earth. Jesus will return *after* the millennium (hence *post*millennialism).[14]

3. *Amillennialism* (or *realized millennialism*). The millennium began when Jesus rose from the dead and will conclude

---

12. Cf. Stanley J. Grenz, *The Millennial Maze: Sorting Out Evangelical Options* (Downers Grove, IL: InterVarsity Press, 1992); Darrell L. Bock, ed., *Three Views on the Millennium and Beyond*, Counterpoints (Grand Rapids, MI: Zondervan, 1999).

13. Cf. Michael J. Vlach, *Premillennialism: Why There Must Be a Future Earthly Kingdom of Jesus* (Los Angeles: Theological Studies, 2015); Matt Waymeyer, *Amillennialism and the Age to Come: A Premillennial Critique of the Two-Age Model* (The Woodlands, TX: Kress Biblical Resources, 2016); Sung Wook Chung and David Mathewson, *Models of Premillennialism* (Eugene, OR: Cascade, 2018).

14. Cf. Kenneth L. Gentry Jr., *He Shall Have Dominion: A Postmillennial Eschatology* (Tyler, TX: Institute for Christian Economics, 1992); Keith A. Mathison, *Postmillennialism: An Eschatology of Hope* (Phillipsburg, NJ: P&R, 1999); Peter J. Leithart, *Revelation*, 2 vols., The International Theological Commentary on the Holy Scripture of the Old and New Testaments (London: Bloomsbury T&T Clark, 2018), 2:298–310.

when he returns to earth. Believers who die during this period reign with King Jesus in heaven. When Jesus died and rose again, he decisively defeated Satan and "bound him" (Rev. 20:2–3; cf. Matt. 12:28–29; John 12:31–32). At the end of this age, Satan will furiously attempt to attack God's people one last time (Rev. 20:7–10).[15]

It's interesting to consider which of those three views is most plausible. For decades I was convinced of premillennialism, but over the past decade I gave premillennialism only a slight edge over amillennialism. Now I think amillennialism is a little more plausible than premillennialism, and I think both are far more plausible than postmillennialism—though I wish postmillennialism were true!

But your millennial view isn't that important.[16] What's far more important is that *Jesus is coming back to slay the dragon and save his bride!* Whatever it means that an angel binds the dragon for a thousand years, we can agree that, at minimum, it entails that *God is more powerful than the dragon.* The dragon cannot bind God, but God can send one of his angels to bind Satan.

The Dragon Attempts to Deceive the Nations

And he seized the dragon, that ancient serpent, who is the devil and Satan, and bound him for a thousand years, and threw him into the pit, and shut it and sealed it over him, *so that he might not deceive the nations any longer, until the*

---

15. Cf. Beale, *Revelation*, 972–1031; Sam Storms, *Kingdom Come: The Amillennial Alternative* (Fearn, Scotland: Mentor, 2013).

16. The professors and pastors with whom I serve hold variations of all three views, and we get along just fine! Using the model of theological triage, one's millennial view should not be a cardinal doctrine (i.e., a teaching that is most central and essential to Christianity—what is "of first importance" [1 Cor. 15:3]) or a denominational distinctive (i.e., an important teaching that creates reasonable boundaries between local churches) but is a nonessential teaching that is a disputable matter. Cf. Andrew David Naselli, *How to Understand and Apply the New Testament: Twelve Steps from Exegesis to Theology* (Phillipsburg, NJ: P&R, 2017), 295–96; Gavin Ortlund, *Finding the Right Hills to Die On: The Case for Theological Triage* (Wheaton, IL: Crossway, 2020).

thousand years were ended. After that he must be released for a little while. . . .

And when the thousand years are ended, *Satan will be released from his prison and will come out to deceive the nations* that are at the four corners of the earth, Gog and Magog, to gather them for battle; their number is like the sand of the sea. And they marched up over the broad plain of the earth and surrounded the camp of the saints and the beloved city, but fire came down from heaven and consumed them, and the devil *who had deceived them* was thrown into the lake of fire and sulfur where the beast and the false prophet were, and they will be tormented day and night forever and ever. (Rev. 20:2–3, 7–10)

The dragon is the ancient serpent—the devil and Satan. Thus, the dragon is "the deceiver of the whole world" (Rev. 12:9). He attempts to deceive the nations to destroy God's people (20:3, 7, 10).[17]

The Dragon Is Tormented Forever in the Lake of Fire and Sulfur

But fire came down from heaven and consumed them, and *the devil who had deceived them was thrown into the lake of fire and sulfur* where the beast and the false prophet were, and they will be *tormented day and night forever and ever.* (Rev. 20:9–10)

Never again will the dragon, that ancient serpent, accuse or deceive or persecute God's people. The dragon will consciously experience fiery torment forever.[18] God will sovereignly and perfectly

---

17. If amillennialism is correct, then the battle in Rev. 20:7–10 is the same battle as in 16:13–16 and 19:17–21. The book is not in strict chronological order; it repeats certain events and focuses on a different aspect of the event in each instance.

18. Cf. D. A. Carson, "On Banishing the Lake of Fire," in *The Gagging of God: Christianity Confronts Pluralism* (Grand Rapids, MI: Zondervan, 1996), 515–36; Christopher W. Morgan

enforce justice—justice for which God's people now yearn and for which God's people will eternally praise God.

Conclusion

One major purpose of the last book of the Bible is to comfort and encourage Christians by revealing future events and providing a heavenly perspective on present earthly difficulties. You could subtitle the book of Revelation as *The Return of the King*. We might quibble over how to interpret various details in the book, but the theological message is clear: *the Lamb will consummate his kingdom for God's glory by slaying the dragon and saving his bride.*

At the beginning of Genesis, when the snake tempts Eve, sin and death enter the world and God banishes humans from his presence. At the end of Revelation, God conquers the dragon, banishes sin, destroys death, and lives among his people in the Most Holy Place, the worldwide garden.[19]

and Robert A. Peterson, eds., *Hell under Fire: Modern Scholarship Reinvents Eternal Punishment* (Grand Rapids, MI: Zondervan, 2004).

19. Cf. Jason S. DeRouchie, Oren R. Martin, and Andrew David Naselli, *40 Questions about Biblical Theology*, 40 Questions (Grand Rapids, MI: Kregel, 2020), question 35: "How Do Genesis 1–3 and Revelation 21–22 Relate as the Bible's Bookends?"

Conclusion

Living in Light of the Story of the
Serpent and the Serpent Slayer

Sometimes the hardest theological question to answer is "So what?" Jesus is the serpent slayer. So how should a Christian live in light of that thrilling storyline? I'll suggest six ways.

Don't Imitate the Poisonous Serpent

The serpent's offspring imitate the serpent.

> You are of your father the devil, and your will is to do your father's desires. He was a murderer from the beginning, and does not stand in the truth, because there is no truth in him. When he lies, he speaks out of his own character, for he is a liar and the father of lies. (John 8:44)

According to Jesus, you imitate the poisonous serpent when you (1) murder, (2) reject the truth, and (3) lie. For example, (1) killing unborn babies imitates the devouring dragon;[1] (2) embracing the

---

1. Cf. Scott Klusendorf, *The Case for Life: Equipping Christians to Engage the Culture* (Wheaton, IL: Crossway, 2009).

prosperity gospel imitates the deceptive snake;[2] (3) and slandering people by gossiping about them imitates the poisonous serpent.[3]

The snake and his offspring deceive people with *words*. God's people must not imitate the poisonous serpent by how they use their tongues.

> The tongue is a fire, a world of unrighteousness. The tongue is set among our members, staining the whole body, setting on fire the entire course of life, and set on fire by hell. For every kind of beast and bird, of reptile and sea creature, can be tamed and has been tamed by mankind, but no human being can tame the tongue. It is a restless evil, *full of deadly poison*. With it we bless our Lord and Father, and with it we curse people who are made in the likeness of God. From the same mouth come blessing and cursing. My brothers, these things ought not to be so. (James 3:6–10)

You imitate the poisonous serpent when you curse a fellow human being, who bears God's image. "The whole law is fulfilled in one word: 'You shall love your neighbor as yourself.' But if you bite and devour one another, watch out that you are not consumed by one another" (Gal. 5:14–15).

Christians can sin by imitating the serpent. The apostle Peter illustrates two ways.

1. A Christian can sin by deceiving others to believe what is false. Peter sinned that way when he separated himself from Gentile Christians. When he behaved out of step with the gospel, he misled other Jewish Christians, including Barnabas (Gal. 2). We imitate the serpent when we lead others to sin (cf. Matt. 18:6).

---

2. Cf. David W. Jones and Russell S. Woodbridge, *Health, Wealth and Happiness: Has the Prosperity Gospel Overshadowed the Gospel of Christ?* (Grand Rapids, MI: Kregel, 2011). See also the documentary *American Gospel: Christ Alone* (Transition Studios, 2018).

3. Cf. Matthew C. Mitchell, *Resisting Gossip: Winning the War of the Wagging Tongue* (Fort Washington, PA: CLC, 2013).

2. A Christian can sin by thinking he or she is better than God in some way—smarter, wiser, more powerful, more righteous. Peter sinned that way when he rebuked Jesus for prophesying about his death and resurrection. Jesus replied to Peter, "Get behind me, *Satan!* You are a hindrance to me. For you are not setting your mind on the things of God, but on the things of man" (Matt. 16:23).

Beware of the Serpent as the Deceiving Snake and Devouring Dragon

Be sober-minded; be watchful. Your adversary the devil prowls around like a roaring lion, seeking someone to devour. (1 Pet. 5:8)

Here God describes Satan not as the deceiving snake or devouring dragon but as a roaring lion, which conveys basically the same idea as a devouring dragon. Satan is not your friend. He does not have your best interest in mind. Satan is hunting you. You are Satan's prey. He sneaks around to find people like you to devour.

So beware! Be on guard. Expect him to attack and to keep attacking. Don't let your guard down. And don't flirt with the serpent by entertaining his ear-tickling lies.[4]

For example, the deceiving snake might tempt you to indulge in pornography. When the serpent tempts you, he doesn't say something like this:

---

4. For what that might look like in modern times, see C. S. Lewis, *The Screwtape Letters: With Screwtape Proposes a Toast* (New York: Touchstone, 1996). Cf. Andrew David Naselli, "Diabolical Ventriloquism: A 1-Sentence Summary of Each of Screwtape's Letters," Thoughts on Theology, July 25, 2013, http://andynaselli.com/diabolical-ventriloquism-a-1-sentence-summary-of-each -of-screwtapes-letters. See also Lewis, *The Pilgrim's Regress: An Allegorical Apology for Christianity, Reason, and Romanticism*, 3rd ed. (Grand Rapids, MI: Eerdmans, 1943). Lewis wisely begins his preface to *The Screwtape Letters* by cautioning readers: "There are two equal and opposite errors into which our race can fall about the devils. One is to disbelieve in their existence. The other is to believe, and to feel an excessive and unhealthy interest in them. They themselves are equally pleased by both errors and hail a materialist or a magician with the same delight" (*Screwtape Letters*, ix). See John R. Gilhooly, *40 Questions about Angels, Demons, and Spiritual Warfare*, 40 Questions (Grand Rapids, MI: Kregel, 2018).

I've run a cost-benefit analysis for you regarding whether you should indulge in pornography. The *benefit* is that you may feel some immediate pleasure, a little buzz. But the *cost* is at least sevenfold: (1) It may send you to hell. (2) It does not glorify God with your body. (3) It is a poisonous, fleeting pleasure. (4) It foolishly wastes your life. (5) It betrays your spouse and children. (6) It ruins your mind and conscience. (7) It participates in sex slavery. What do you think is the wiser choice?[5]

Satan never tempts people that way. He tempts with lies. He tempts you to think that you would be happier without God, without submitting to God as your gracious master.

The imagery of snakes and dragons should shock you out of spiritual slumber so that you see the world as it really is.[6] Satan really is a deceiving snake and a devouring dragon.[7] He is scheming to deceive and destroy you with false teaching. He wants you to believe what is false.

So beware of the deceiving snake and devouring dragon. "It does not do," J. R. R. Tolkien reminds us in *The Hobbit*, "to leave a live dragon out of your calculations, if you live near him."[8]

---

5. Cf. Andrew David Naselli, "Seven Reasons You Should Not Indulge in Pornography," *Themelios* 41, no. 3 (2016): 473–83.

6. Cf. G. K. Beale, "The Purpose of Symbolism in the Book of Revelation," *Calvin Theological Journal* 41, no. 1 (2006): 53–66.

7. Cf. Tony Reinke, *Lit! A Christian Guide to Reading Books* (Wheaton, IL: Crossway, 2011), 81–89.

8. J. R. R. Tolkien, *The Hobbit: or, There and Back Again* (Boston: Houghton Mifflin, 1937), 199. Here's the fuller context of that pithy advice:

> The dwarves were still passing the cup from hand to hand and talking delightedly of the recovery of their treasure, when suddenly a vast rumbling woke in the mountain underneath as if it was an old volcano that had made up its mind to start eruptions once again. The door behind them was pulled nearly to, and blocked from closing with a stone, but up the long tunnel came the dreadful echoes, from far down in the depths, of a bellowing and a trampling that made the ground beneath them tremble. Then the dwarves forgot their joy and their confident boasts of a moment before and cowered down in fright. Smaug was still to be reckoned with. It does not do to leave a live dragon out of your calculations, if you live near him. (199)

Fight the Serpent as the Deceiving Snake and Devouring Dragon

For though we walk in the flesh, *we are not waging war according to the flesh. For the weapons of our warfare are not of the flesh but have divine power to destroy strongholds. We destroy arguments and every lofty opinion raised against the knowledge of God,* and take every thought captive to obey Christ, being ready to punish every disobedience, when your obedience is complete. (2 Cor. 10:3–6)

Be angry and do not sin; do not let the sun go down on your anger, and *give no opportunity to the devil* [NIV: "do not give the devil a foothold"]. (Eph. 4:26–27)

Finally, be strong in the Lord and in the strength of his might. *Put on the whole armor of God, that you may be able to stand against the schemes of the devil. For we do not wrestle against flesh and blood, but against the rulers, against the authorities, against the cosmic powers over this present darkness, against the spiritual forces of evil in the heavenly places.* Therefore *take up the whole armor of God, that you may be able to withstand in the evil day, and having done all, to stand firm.* Stand therefore, having fastened on the belt of truth, and having put on the breastplate of righteousness, and, as shoes for your feet, having put on the readiness given by the gospel of peace. In all circumstances take up the shield of faith, with which you can extinguish all the flaming darts of the evil one; and take the helmet of salvation, and *the sword of the Spirit, which is the word of God, praying at all times in the Spirit,* with all prayer and supplication. To that end, *keep alert with all perseverance,* making supplication for all the saints. (Eph. 6:10–18)

Be sober-minded; be watchful. Your adversary the devil prowls around like a roaring lion, seeking someone to devour. *Resist him*, firm in your faith, knowing that the same kinds of suffering are being experienced by your brotherhood throughout the world. (1 Pet. 5:8–9)

Resist the devil, and he will flee from you. (James 4:7)

The serpent is real, and he wants to deceive and devour you. So beware, be alert, wear defensive armor. But that's not all. Don't simply be defensive. Go on the offensive. Fight. Counterattack.

God enables his people to tread on serpents (Ps. 91:13; Luke 10:19; Acts 28:3–4).[9] How? We don't fight the serpent with the same sort of weapons that militaries use to fight battles. We fight the serpent with spiritual weapons such as the ones in Ephesians 6:10–18. We fight the serpent by believing and speaking the truth. By upholding righteousness. By preaching the gospel to ourselves and those around us. By unwaveringly trusting God. By living like what we are—delivered from serving the serpent. By understanding and applying God's word. By praying at all times in the Spirit for ourselves and our brothers and sisters.

We fight the serpent by contending for the faith against grace-perverting immorality (Jude 3–4). By excommunicating false teachers from the church because we recognize them for what they are—intruding snakes. By treasuring what is true and rejecting what is false. By loving what God loves and hating what God hates. By serving as an essential part of our local church's body. By doing good works in our communities by God's grace and in Jesus's name. By refusing to do evil even if serpentine authorities command it—fol-

---

9. Mark 16:18a ("they will pick up serpents with their hands") seems to support that principle, but it's probably not Scripture, since the earliest and best manuscripts do not include it. For details, see the text-critical note on Mark 16:9–20 in the NET Bible. Cf. R. Alan Streett, "Snake Handling and Mark 16:18: Primitive Christianity or Indigenous American Religion?," *Criswell Theological Review* 8, no. 1 (2010): 77–90.

lowing the honorable example of the Hebrew midwives and Moses's parents (Ex. 1; Heb. 11:23).

You won't properly fight the serpent if you are flirting with him. You won't properly fight the serpent if you think he makes some compelling arguments about what is true and what is good. You must be convinced to the core of your being that the serpent is undiluted evil. The serpent is a thief, a murderer, a liar. Jesus spoke the truth about the serpent: "He was a murderer from the beginning, and does not stand in the truth, because there is no truth in him. When he lies, he speaks out of his own character, for he is a liar and the father of lies" (John 8:44). The serpent is the ultimate traitor—he committed treason against the King of the universe. And he is doing everything he can to convince you to commit treason, too.

You won't fight against the serpent the right way unless you *feel* about him the right way. How do you feel about Voldemort when you read *Harry Potter*? How do you feel about Sauron when you read *The Lord of the Rings*? How do you feel about the white witch when you read *The Lion, the Witch, and the Wardrobe*? How do you feel about Apollyon when you read *The Pilgrim's Progress*? That's how you should feel about the serpent in real life. You should feel disgust at his poison, outrage at his injustice, and a deep longing for justice to prevail.[10]

Exult in the Serpent Slayer

How should you feel when you think about what Jesus the serpent slayer has already done to the dragon, and about what the serpent slayer will finally do to the dragon? You should feel elated! You

---

10. For a captivating children's book that creatively supports the first three responses (i.e., don't imitate the poisonous serpent; beware of Satan as the deceiving snake and devouring dragon; and fight Satan as the deceiving snake and devouring dragon), see Marty Machowski, *Dragon Seed* (Greensboro, NC: New Growth, 2017). It targets ages 11–14, but my wife and I along with our younger children loved it when I read it aloud to our family. We also enjoyed a more recent dragon-slaying story appropriate for children: Douglas Wilson, *Andrew and the Firedrake* (Moscow, ID: Canon, 2019).

should fall on your knees to worship the ultimate knight in shining armor, the ultimate dragon slayer.

It's epic when the good guys courageously defeat Sauron or Voldemort. But that's just a shadow compared with the greatest defeat of all time. *Jesus slays the dragon!* If that doesn't make you rejoice, what will? Exult in the serpent slayer.[11]

Enjoy Good Serpent-Slaying Stories as Echoes of the Greatest Story

Good books and films that portray epic stories typically echo the greatest story. Sometimes the antagonist is an actual serpent, but usually the villain is a symbolic serpent that a hero defeats. Learn to enjoy such stories as echoes of the greatest story.

Good stories don't flirt with evil and confuse you about whether good is bad or bad is good. For example, a book or movie that makes your emotions root for a person to commit adultery is sinful. Good stories should make you love what God loves and hate what God hates. The greatest stories do that best.

Perhaps consider creating an epic story yourself that leads others to worship the ultimate serpent slayer. One day you may write a letter similar to one C. S. Lewis wrote to a concerned mother of a son named Laurence:

> Laurence can't *really* love Aslan more than Jesus, even if he feels that's what he is doing. For the things he loves Aslan for doing or saying are simply the things Jesus really did and said. So that when Laurence thinks he is loving Aslan, he is really loving Jesus: and perhaps loving Him more than he ever did before.[12]

---

11. For a children's book (ages 5–12) that exults in the "snake crusher" while concisely summarizing the Bible's storyline, see Kevin DeYoung, *The Biggest Story: How the Snake Crusher Brings Us Back to the Garden* (Wheaton, IL: Crossway, 2015).

12. C. S. Lewis, *The Collected Letters of C. S. Lewis*, ed. Walter Hooper, 3 vols. (San Francisco: HarperSanFrancisco, 2004), 3:603.

Trust the Serpent Slayer

You cannot defeat the serpent on your own. But God is greater than the serpent: "He who is in you is greater than he who is in the world" (1 John 4:4).

There may be times when the serpent is persecuting you or your brothers and sisters in Christ. You may feel afraid, desperate, depressed. That is when you must remember the whole storyline. You know how this story ends! Yes, difficult and tragic events will continue to occur. But you know that the serpent slayer has already decisively defeated the serpent and that at the end he will finally and completely crush the serpent. Don't doubt the serpent slayer's plan, valor, power, or goodness. Trust him. He always does what's right, and in the end we will jubilantly rejoice that Jesus has finally conquered the serpent.

———

Our Father in heaven,
hallowed be your name.
Your kingdom come,
your will be done,
    on earth as it is in heaven.
Give us this day our daily bread,
and forgive us our debts,
    as we also have forgiven our debtors.
And lead us not into temptation,
    but *deliver us from the evil one*. (Matt. 6:9–13)

The Lord is faithful. *He will establish you and guard you against the evil one*. (2 Thess. 3:3)

Appendix

How Often Does the Bible
Explicitly Mention Serpents?

Tracing the serpent theme throughout the Bible's storyline requires locating all the relevant Bible passages. The first step for finding the relevant passages is to locate every word used in reference to a serpent. Sixteen words are most relevant (eleven in the Hebrew Old Testament, five in the Greek New Testament).[1]

1. אֶפְעֶה (*efeh*): "snake." It occurs three times: Job 20:16; Isaiah 30:6; 59:5.
2. לִוְיָתָן (*liwyathan*): "Leviathan, sea monster." Occurs six times: Job 3:8; 40:25 (Eng. 41:1); Psalms 74:14; 104:26; Isaiah 27:1 (2x).
3. נָחָשׁ (*nahash*): "snake [the most common generic word for serpent]." Occurs thirty-one times: Genesis 3:1, 2, 4, 13, 14; 49:17; Exodus 4:3; 7:15; Numbers 21:6, 7, 9 (3x); Deuteronomy 8:15; 2 Kings 18:4; Job 26:13; Psalms 58:5

---

1. Definitions are from Ludwig Koehler, Walter Baumgartner, and Johann Jakob Stamm, *The Hebrew and Aramaic Lexicon of the Old Testament*, ed. and trans. M. E. J. Richardson, 2 vols. (Leiden: Brill, 1994); Walter Bauer et al., eds., *A Greek-English Lexicon of the New Testament and Other Early Christian Literature*, 3rd ed. (Chicago: University of Chicago Press, 2000).

(Eng. 58:4); 140:4 (Eng. 140:3); Proverbs 23:32; 30:19; Ecclesiastes 10:8, 11; Isaiah 14:29; 27:1 (2x); 65:25; Jeremiah 8:17; 46:22; Amos 5:19; 9:3; Micah 7:17.

4. פֶּתֶן (*pethen*): "horned viper [or the Egyptian cobra or uraeus]." Occurs six times: Deuteronomy 32:33; Job 20:14, 16; Psalms 58:5 (Eng. 58:4); 91:13; Isaiah 11:8.

5. צֶפַע (*tsefa*): "poisonous snake, viper." Occurs once: Isaiah 14:29.

6. צִפְעֹנִי (*tsifoni*): "poisonous snake, viper." Occurs four times: Proverbs 23:32; Isaiah 11:8; 59:5; Jeremiah 8:17.

7. עַכְשׁוּב (*akhshuv*): "poisonous horned viper (or adder)." Occurs once: Psalm 140:4 (Eng. 140:3).

8. רַהַב (*rahab*): (1) "mythical monster, the name of which means 'surger' and plays upon the restlessness and crashing of the sea; (2) symbolic designation for Egypt." Occurs seven times: Job 9:13; 26:12; Psalms 40:5 (Eng. 40:4); 87:4; 89:11 (Eng. 89:10); Isaiah 30:7; 51:9.

9. שָׂרָף (*saraph*): "Saraph serpent . . . signifies the color or burning pain of a bite: glowing, burning, or the glowing one, the burning one." Occurs seven times: Numbers 21:6, 8; Deuteronomy 8:15; Isaiah 6:2, 6; 14:29; 30:6.

10. שְׁפִיפֹן (*shephiphon*): "horned viper." Occurs once: Genesis 49:17.

11. תַּנִּין (*tannin*): "(1a) sea-monster, sea-dragon; (1b) dragon; (2a) serpent; (2b) crocodile. The hypothetical form תַּן (*tan*) means *jackal*." Occurs fourteen times: Genesis 1:21; Exodus 7:9, 10, 12; Deuteronomy 32:33; Job 7:12; Psalms 74:13; 91:13; 148:7; Isaiah 27:1; 51:9; Jeremiah 51:34; Ezekiel 29:3; 32:2.

12. ἀσπίς (*aspis*): "asp, Egyptian cobra, generally of venomous snakes." Occurs once: Romans 3:13.

13. δράκων (*drakōn*): "*dragon, serpent,* a sobriquet [i.e., nickname] for the devil." Occurs thirteen times: Revelation 12:3, 4, 7 (2x), 9, 13, 16, 17; 13:2, 4, 11; 16:13; 20:2.

14. ἑρπετόν (*herpeton*): "*reptile.*" Occurs four times: Acts 10:12; 11:6; Romans 1:23; James 3:7.

15. ἔχιδνα (*echidna*): "*snake,* our texts do not permit identification of species, but the term ordinarily suggests a poisonous one: probably *Vipera ammodytes,* commonly known as sand viper." Occurs five times: Matthew 3:7; 12:34; 23:33; Luke 3:7; Acts 28:3.

16. ὄφις (*ophis*): "(1) a limbless reptile, *snake, serpent;* (2) a person perceived as dangerous, *snake;* (3) a symbolic figure, frequent in mythology, *serpent.*" Occurs thirteen times: Matthew 7:10; 10:16; 23:33; Luke 10:19; 11:11; John 3:14; 1 Corinthians 10:9; 2 Corinthians 11:3; Revelation 9:19; 12:9, 14, 15; 20:2 (also Mark 16:18).

Figures 1 and 2 display how many times the above Hebrew and Greek words appear in *books* of the Bible.

Figure 1. Occurrences of Hebrew terms for serpent *in Old Testament books*

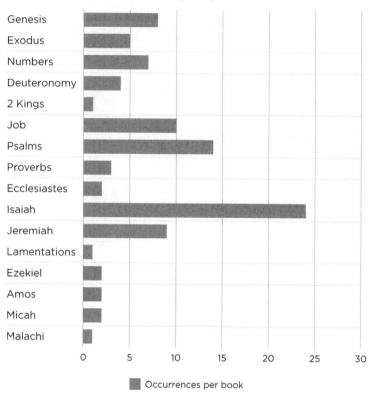

Occurrences per book

Figure 2. Occurrences of Greek terms for serpent *in New Testament books*

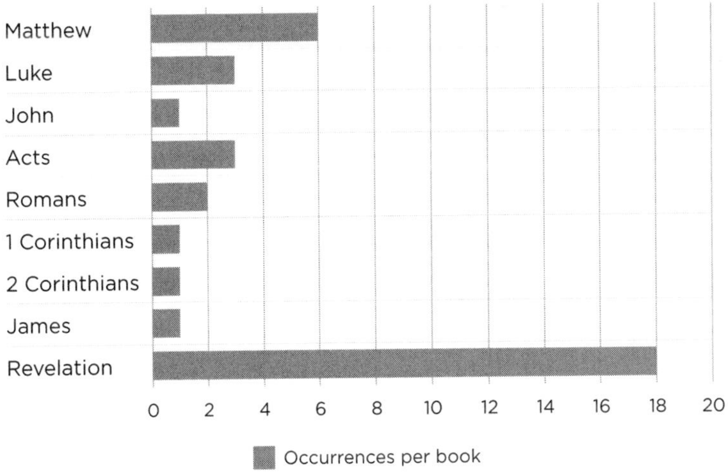

Figures 3 and 4 display how many times the above Hebrew and Greek words appear in *chapters* of the Bible.

Figure 3. Occurrences of Hebrew terms for serpent *in Old Testament chapters*

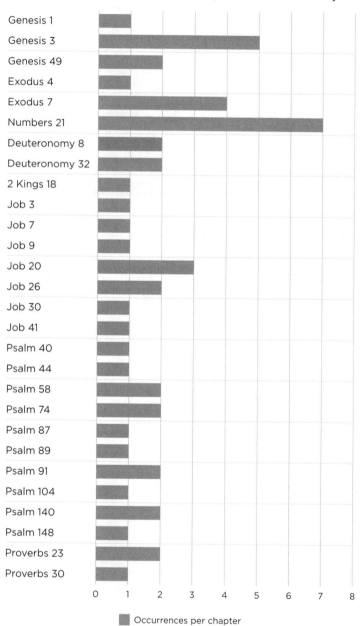

Figure 3. (continued)

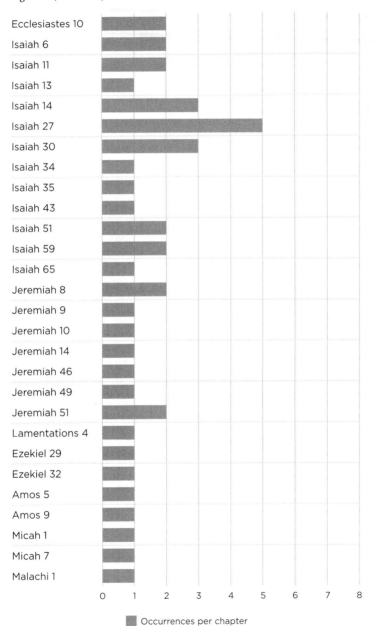

Occurrences per chapter

Figure 4. Occurrences of Greek terms for serpent *in New Testament chapters*

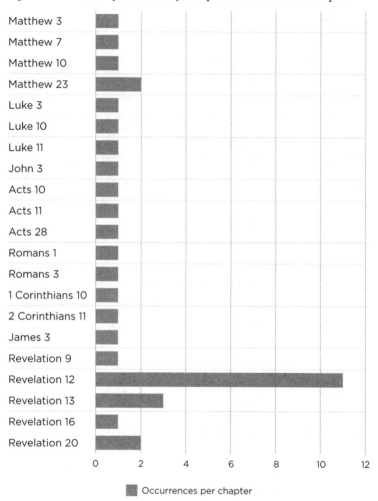

Occurrences per chapter

The four graphs are especially helpful for displaying that serpent terms occur most frequently in Isaiah and Revelation. But one must be careful not to draw incorrect inferences from the graphs. Two inferences in particular are incorrect.

1. It is incorrect to infer that the above passages are *all* of the relevant passages. Locating all of the passages that use terms for serpent is necessary to finding relevant passages, but it is not sufficient because sometimes a passage may address the serpent topic without using a serpent word. For example, "I will send the teeth of beasts against them, with *the venom of things that crawl in the dust*" (Deut. 32:24).

2. It is incorrect to infer that the books or chapters with few occurrences are insignificant. Job 41, for example, has only one occurrence of Leviathan, but the entire chapter is about Leviathan.

General Index

Scripture Index

Short Studies in
Biblical Theology Series

THE SON OF GOD
AND THE NEW CREATION

GRAEME GOLDSWORTHY

MARRIAGE
AND THE MYSTERY OF THE GOSPEL

RAY ORTLUND

WORK
AND OUR LABOR IN THE LORD

JAMES M. HAMILTON JR.

COVENANT
AND GOD'S PURPOSE FOR THE WORLD

THOMAS R. SCHREINER

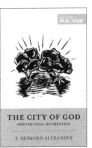

THE CITY OF GOD
AND THE GOAL OF CREATION

T. DESMOND ALEXANDER

THE KINGDOM OF GOD
AND THE GLORY OF THE CROSS

PATRICK SCHREINER

FROM CHAOS TO COSMOS
CREATION TO NEW CREATION

SIDNEY GREIDANUS

THE LORD'S SUPPER
AS THE SIGN AND MEAL OF THE NEW COVENANT

GUY PRENTISS WATERS

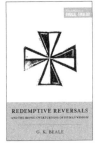

REDEMPTIVE REVERSALS
AND THE IRONIC OVERTURNING OF HUMAN WISDOM

G. K. BEALE

DIVINE BLESSING
AND THE FULLNESS OF LIFE IN THE PRESENCE OF GOD

WILLIAM R. OSBORNE

THE SERPENT
AND THE SERPENT SLAYER

ANDREW DAVID NASELLI

For more information, visit **crossway.org/ssbt**.